Successful Foreign Acquisitions
The Pivotal Role of the Management Accountant

Professor Tony Appleyard and Simon Pallett
University of Newcastle upon Tyne

AMSTERDAM • BOSTON • HEIDELBERG • LONDON • NEW YORK
OXFORD • PARIS • SAN DIEGO • SAN FRANCISCO • SINGAPORE
SYDNEY • TOKYO

CIMA Publishing is an imprint of Elsevier

Acknowledgements

The support of the CIMA Research Foundation under its initiative, Management Accounting and Control in Different International Environments, is gratefully acknowledged.

The authors also acknowledge the help received from numerous managerial and accounting staff in the companies visited, who not only gave freely and generously of their time, but also were generous in their hospitality. For reasons of confidentiality, they must remain anonymous.

Thanks too to Thomas Ahrens of the LSE for advice on technical issues to do with German accounting and to two anonymous referees for their helpful comments.

CIMA Publishing
An imprint of Elsevier
Linacre House, Jordan Hill, Oxford OX2 8DP
200 Wheeler Road, Burlington, MA 01803

First published 2004

Permissions may be sought directly from Elsevier's Science and Technology Rights Department in Oxford, UK: phone: (+44) (0) 1865 843830; fax: (+44) (0) 1865 853333; e-mail: permissions@elsevier.co.uk. You may also complete your request on-line via the Elsevier homepage (http://www.elsevier.com), by selecting 'Customer Support' and then 'Obtaining Permissions'

British Library Cataloguing in Publication Data
A catalogue record for this book is available from the British Library

ISBN 0 7506 6172 0

For information on all CIMA Publishing publications
visit our website at www.cimapublishing.com

Printed and bound in Great Britain

Contents

Executive Summary   v

1   Introduction   1

2   Literature Review – Anglo-German Differences   5
    2.1   GAAP   7
    2.2   The accounting profession   9
    2.3   The concept of cost in Germany   10
    2.4   Culture   12
    2.5   Capital markets   15
    2.6   Corporate governance   16
    2.7   Co-determination   17
    2.8   German managers, organisational structure and rewards   19

3   Literature Review – the Acquisitions Process   21

4   The Research Framework   27

5   Case Study One – UK Parent and German Subsidiary   31
    5.1   Background information on the companies and the strategic motivation for the acquisition   33
    5.2   Analysis of the acquisition strategy   34
    5.3   UKP's management control system and implementing the strategy   37
    5.4   Review of the actual management control system   41
    5.5   Culture: Anglo-German differences   49
    5.6   Conclusions   53

6   Case Study Two – German Parent and UK Subsidiary   57
    6.1   Background information on the companies and the strategic motivation for the acquisition   59
    6.2   Analysis of the acquisition strategy   61
    6.3   The management control system and implementing the strategy   62
    6.4   Review of the actual management control system   64
    6.5   Budgetary control   69
    6.6   Incentive arrangements   74
    6.7   Culture: Anglo-German differences   76
    6.8   Conclusions   77

7   Discussion and Conclusions   81
7.1   Corporate strategy and management accounting   83
7.2   Initial organisational control   83
7.3   Achieving effective control   84
7.4   Management accounting in cross-border acquisitions   84
7.5   Foreign exchange issues   85
7.6   Culture   87

8   Lessons to be Learnt from the Case Studies   91

9   References   97

Appendices   103
Appendix 1 – Sources of Information about Germany   105
Appendix 2 – DM:£ spot (mid) quarterly exchange rate
                        (1991–98)   106
Appendix 3 – Personnel Interviewed   107
Appendix 4 – Budgetary Control at UKP and GS   109
Appendix 5 – The Finance Function at GP   112

Index   113

Executive Summary

Terms of reference

This research investigated two cross-border acquisitions, one of a German subsidiary by a British parent, and the other of a British subsidiary by a German parent, with the aim of looking at the role of management accounting in the process and trying to draw lessons about the acquisition and integration process that would be useful to practitioners. The implicit model used in the analysis is as follows:

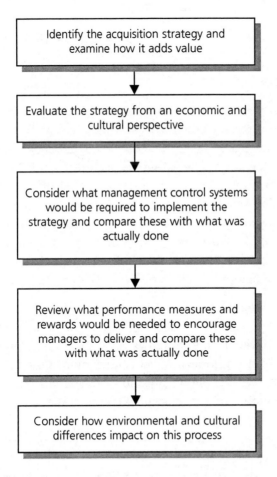

The analytical model of acquisition and management control

This research was carried out principally by means of semi-structured interviews with accounting and management staff in both parent and subsidiary. The interviews were supplemented by the study of company documents and accounting reports. Interviewees were asked about the rationale for the acquisition, problems in making it work, perceived Anglo-German differences, the structure of the business, budgetary control, IT systems, costing, capital expenditure control and a range of accounting issues. They were also asked how they, with the benefit of hindsight, would do things differently if they were to go through the process again, or, in other words, what lessons they had learnt.

Background to the two cases

The two cases differ in some important respects.

Case study one

Case study one concerns a large quoted UK manufacturing company which acquired a German subsidiary in 1991 with the aim of diversifying away from dependence on the UK market and achieving some vertical integration. The subsidiary acquired is small in relation to the group, but large in relation to the specialist division in which it is located. The acquired company has suffered quite severe problems in achieving good performance and in providing its parent with timely and relevant information in the form the parent requires. It has taken years to sort out these problems, and, in particular, to install successfully a computerised standard costing module.

Key to making progress has been the appointment of a new managing director, a German who had worked for the group previously, and a new controller. This case shows some significant Anglo-German differences in the approach to accounting and in the role and status of accounting within the organisation, both of which impact upon the implementation of a management control system.

Case study two

Case study two involves a quoted German group in project engineering which tried to acquire a UK company in the same line of business, but was beaten to it by a competitor. Instead it acquired the people with expertise and bought a UK repairs and maintenance company, combining the two to form its UK subsidiary. It needed a UK presence because of the rather nationalistic character of purchasing in its industry.

The repairs and maintenance business provided a useful complement to the mainstream project business, because there were some synergies. The company is essentially in the business of selling its technical expertise and has relatively few staff compared to the group in case study one. The German parent did experience problems with its UK subsidiary in terms of achieving acceptable profits; indeed without the parent's support the UK company might not have survived. Accounting issues did not figure as a significant cause of difficulty, partly because the accounting systems inherited were so weak that the company just started again from scratch. However, as in case study one the key to progress was the installation of a new managing director by the parent, in this case a German with experience of the industry, who had recently been taken on by the parent in another capacity.

Findings

The principal findings are as follows:

1. Both case studies had a clearly defined acquisition strategy which suggested that the acquisition would add value to the business.
2. In case study one the strategy was one of capturing gains from vertical integration. However, an analysis of the economics suggested that there were doubts about any value creation. In case study two, world-wide deregulation of the industry created an opportunity for a global strategy of growth and profitability. It also acquired technical expertise to improve its products. It should have been successful.
3. There were possible management control system solutions for case study one but the lack of value may explain the inertia in developing an appropriate management control system to make it happen. Instead management accounting differences and problems were seen by UK parent managers to be a significant factor in the UK parent company's difficulties in making a success of the acquisition. This arose because the UK acquirer attempted to implement its standard costing system in the German subsidiary without any regard to whether it was appropriate and failed to understand the role and status of the finance function, how man-

agement accounting data was used and what was measured. This could be interpreted as a cultural dimension. For example, the German management accounting function was not as product-focused as the UK parent required and there were differences in relation to the use of estimates and simpler methods, with the Germans keen to do things in a strictly correct way regardless of complexity or the value added by precision. In case study two however, the lack of well-implemented management control system delayed the successful realisation of the strategy. Management accounting was not perceived as a barrier to the successful implementation of the strategy.

4. In both cases subsidiaries were allowed considerable autonomy in how they did their accounting within the constraints of delivering standard reports. This compromised cost comparisons, which were essential for both parents given their competitive environment and the need for cost leadership.

5. Both parents failed to institute adequate control, relying on periodic visits to achieve their objectives. Neither realised in advance how large an investment of managerial time was going to be required and neither planned to make that resource available as part of its acquisition strategy.

6. In both case studies, subsidiaries operated local currency budgets and managers did not need to be concerned at all about translation gains and losses, although these did impact on final group profit. They faced no pressure to alter their behaviour to respond to such influences, since rewards were (substantially) based on local currency budgets. Subsidiary managers did have to deal with transaction exposure and were left to arrange hedging themselves. Despite the benefits which might arise from centralising foreign exchange risk management, the groups did not do this, perhaps on grounds of administrative simplicity. Although the impact of foreign exchange movements on competitiveness would be used to explain variances from budget, there were no formal mechanisms for adjusting budget targets or managerial incentives. The basic picture therefore is of simple rather than sophisticated systems being employed to address the impact of foreign exchange movements.

7. Although the two case studies are very different, there is a common thread of underachievement and failure to meet targets, caused more by managerial failings than accounting problems. In both cases, imposing new managers – done some years later – was key to secur-

ing improvements and instituting proper management controls. However, there are potential problems with new managers because of language, lack of local expertise and the loss of local knowledge.

8. Language is a difference that affects UK companies buying subsidiaries abroad more than it affects German companies making a UK acquisition. Managers in German companies that operate internationally have to speak English, which gives them an advantage in managing UK and US subsidiaries.

9. Differences in business culture, GAAP, labour markets and capital markets have to be taken into account by managers operating abroad, but none of these represent fundamental obstacles to operating a foreign subsidiary successfully. They are simply areas where the managers concerned need good briefings and need to be prepared to learn. The differences matter and have to be coped with. Serious mistakes could be made by managers ignorant of them, but they should not represent a serious long-term problem.

10. It is not necessary for there to be common IT systems but a common communication package is essential.

What was largely missing from the case studies was the role of the management accountant in:

◆ evaluating and clarifying the strategy
◆ communicating it throughout the business so that the managers share the vision
◆ determining what management control systems are required to realise the acquisition strategy
◆ determining what investment of managerial resource by the parent is needed to get to understand fully the subsidiary and to implement the desired control procedures
◆ inspecting existing management accounting arrangements and making the changes needed to meet the group's reporting and control requirements
◆ evaluating the quality of key management and accounting personnel

Finally the analytical model used by the authors and shown in diagrammatic form at the beginning of this section works well as an analytical tool, explaining the cases satisfactorily. Furthermore, it provides the basis of a model which practitioners might use when making a foreign acquisition.

Introduction

This research was carried out under CIMA's initiative to support research proposals concerned with management accounting and control in different international environments. The CIMA Research Foundation awarded the authors a grant to carry out two in-depth case studies on the management accounting implications of absorbing a new foreign subsidiary. The authors were aware of a British company, which appeared to have had quite severe problems, especially in the management accounting area, with a German company it had acquired, and of a German parent with a British subsidiary it had acquired. Both companies agreed to take part in the research project subject to the companies and individual interviewees remaining anonymous.

Case studies enjoy a clear comparative advantage over other methods of research in terms of context and depth. Semi-structured interviews allow the researcher to explore issues which emerge and to gain significant insights into issues of day-to-day management and accounting. However, there are problems. Case studies are reliant on memory, sometimes for events which occurred some time ago, they are dependent on a small number of interviewees, and there is a risk of bias (Jones, 1985). As far as possible, the authors countered this by seeking confirmation from written documents, by providing interviewees with advance warning of the areas of questioning so that they could prepare and refresh their memories and by asking the same questions of more than one person.

Germany appeared to be an interesting country to choose, since it offered a strong contrast to the UK in a number of significant respects, which will be explored in Chapter 2. The project's ability to look at the issue from both sides – a German parent with a UK subsidiary and a UK parent with a subsidiary in Germany – offered a useful opportunity to study the area from both German and British perspectives.

In this report the companies will be referred to as follows:

- ◆ a UK parent as UKP;
- ◆ its German subsidiary as GS;
- ◆ a German parent as GP;
- ◆ its UK subsidiary as UKS.

The report is structured as follows:

- ◆ Chapter 2 provides a literature review on key Anglo-German differences in accounting and business. It provides useful factual background, as well as providing a theoretical framework against which actual findings can be tested.

◆ Chapter 3 reviews the literature on the management of acquired companies and on the management of foreign acquisitions, so as to provide a theoretical framework for this dimension.

◆ Chapter 4 provides the analytical framework for evaluating the case studies.

◆ Chapters 5 and 6 contain the two case studies, starting with an anonymised factual background, the acquisition strategy and its evaluation. The analysis then moves on to look at what management control systems and incentive arrangements would have been required to implement the strategy successfully, and compares these with what actually happened. Each case study also looks at perceived Anglo-German differences and what lessons can be learned from the acquisition as reported by the interviewees, before drawing some conclusions. As far as possible, a common format is used, but some issues arose in only one of the case studies.

◆ Chapter 7 provides a discussion of the general findings from the project.

◆ Chapter 8 provides a brief summary of the main lessons to be learned for other firms undertaking acquisitions abroad.

◆ References and several appendices follow at the end.

Literature Review –
Anglo-German Differences

This chapter provides some background on Anglo-German differences in accounting and in other areas of business life. It provides the necessary context for the case studies, as well as providing material that would, in its own right, be interesting for companies doing business in Germany or with German subsidiaries. Commentary will be limited to areas which are particularly relevant to the case studies, since it is not the purpose of the chapter to provide a comprehensive catalogue of all Anglo-German differences in accounting and business. For a comprehensive list of sources of information on Anglo-German differences see Appendix 1.

The key accounting and business differences are presented in Table 2.1. An analysis of these differences then follows. This addresses how such differences might be expected to impact on the strategy of a cross-border acquisition and on the implementation of the management control systems needed to make the strategy work.

In 1998, Germany set up an accounting standards body independent of government but recognised by the Ministry of Justice, whose role is to advise parliament, represent Germany on international bodies and develop a set of standards for consolidated accounts (Deutsche Rechnungslegungs Standards Committee, 2000). It aims to achieve greater flexibility than a legally based system can achieve, but its role is limited to the group accounts of large German companies, which need to produce internationally acceptable financial statements in order to raise finance abroad.

2.1 GAAP

The differential impact of financial reporting rules on management accounting is of relevance to the case studies examined here, particularly as it feeds through into performance measures and costing systems. In general, GAAP differences will create additional accounting costs often for very little benefit. There are two issues:

2.1.1 Matching v prudence

UK GAAP gives priority to matching, Germany gives priority to prudence. German GAAP (and tax rules) applies strict historical cost but permits provisions for anticipated losses where UK (or US) GAAP would not recognise a liability. The main effects are:

Table 2.1: Summary of Anglo-German differences as at December 1999

Area	UK	Germany
Financial reporting – underlying causes of difference	• Low level of legal rules for accounting • Importance of the stock market • Little tax influence • Large and influential profession	• Code law system with most accounting rules enshrined in law • Stock market much less important • Strong tax influence on financial reporting • Smaller and less influential profession
Significant GAAP differences	• Modified historical cost • Fair depreciation • Percentage of completion method for long-term contracts • Limited scope to make provisions	• Strict historical cost • Accelerated depreciation driven by tax • Profit on long-term contracts only recognised on completion • Greater scope for making provisions and smoothing profit
Accounting profession	• Large • Many different professional bodies • Professional route to training for management accountants • Influential in UK companies	• Smaller profession • Main body is for practising auditors only • Management accountants are business economics graduates but do not undergo professional training • Less influential in German companies where engineers dominate
Management accounting	• Management accounting tends to use same measurement bases as financial reporting	• Long history of using different measurement bases from financial accounting
Hofstede's cultural dimensions	• More individual • Low uncertainty avoidance	• More collectivist • High uncertainty avoidance
Gray's cultural dimensions*	• Professionalism • Flexible rather than uniform • Optimistic • High level of transparency	• Statutory control • Strong elements of flexibility • Prudent • Lower disclosures
Capital markets	• 2400 listed companies, 1998 • Shareholdings generally dispersed and dominated by financial institutions	• 700 listed companies, 1998 • Banks play a more significant role • Lot of large shareholdings and dominated by industrial and commercial companies
Corporate governance	• Unitary board • Worker representation not found	• Management board and supervisory board • Worker representation mandatory
Co-determination	• Works councils not usual	• Works council required by law and with rights to be consulted
Managers	• Finance dominates • Generalist managers • Bonuses tied to profitability • Stock options common	• Engineering dominates • Technical specialists • Broader bonus criteria • Stock options rare

- **provisions** create the opportunity to smooth income or performance, with provisions no longer required written back to the profit and loss under the heading Other Income (Haskins, Ferris and Selling, 1996);
- **long-term work in progress** – prudence allows no anticipation of the profit in advance of completion;
- **depreciation** charges in Germany are usually based on the tax rules rather than the expected useful life of the asset.

2.1.2 Disclosure

The key points are as follows:

- Traditionally, German disclosure has been less transparent. For example, there is less detailed segment reporting and many disclosures which are obligatory for listed UK companies are, or have been, voluntary for their German counterparts (e.g. earnings per share (EPS), cash-flow statements). Cash-flow statements became compulsory for listed companies only as of 1 January 1999 (Seckler, 1998).
- Large German companies voluntarily disclose more information. Since 1993, some large listed German companies have started voluntarily to prepare group accounts under IAS or US GAAP.
- In 1998, the German parliament passed laws (*Accountancy International*, 1998) to allow listed companies needing access to foreign capital markets to use IAS or US GAAP for their group accounts, thus freeing them from the obligation to produce group accounts in compliance with the HGB (the Handelsgesetzbuch which is part of the Commercial Code);
- Filing requirements for smaller private companies are easily avoided by the payment of a modest fine and surveys have shown very low levels of compliance (Ordelheide and Pfaff, 1994);
- The Fourth and Seventh EU Directives provide a basic common framework for disclosure.

2.2 The accounting profession

The accounting profession in Germany is much smaller and less influential than the very large UK profession and is different in its nature. The main German professional body, the Institut der Wirtschaftsprüfer, is a body for auditors in professional practice only and therefore differs from the UK Institute of Chartered Accountants.

There is no German professional body for management accountants, i.e. no equivalent of the Chartered Institute of Management Accountants (CIMA). Some management accountants will belong to the Controller Verein (Controllers Association), but this is a voluntary association and not one where members have achieved professional examinations and approved work experience. Essentially, staff in Germany working in the management accounting area will either have come to their posts via an apprenticeship or will have been recruited straight from university. Business Economics (Betriebswirtschaftslehre), which includes some accounting, is the subject most German management accountants will have studied at university. It is also possible to go to university after doing an apprenticeship and the Controller in GS in case study one had followed this route.

The absence of a professional body, Scherrer (1996) argues, makes academic commentators more important. It may also make management accountants more academic or theoretical in their outlook (Ahrens, 1996, 1997a, 1997b). Ahrens has reported that management accountants are not as influential in German companies as they are in the UK and this affects their role. They will be much less involved in the strategic management process or the day-to-day business; they will not challenge decisions made by other professionals and intervene in operational matters even for common procedures such as budget formulation. Their role is to provide information for other functions whose role it is to make decisions. Where cross-border acquisitions had taken place, Ahrens found that the British management accountants could not understand what function their German colleagues were fulfilling, whilst the German management accountants felt that their British colleagues meddled too much in operational matters.

These differences turned out to be more relevant in the first case study – the acquisition of a German subsidiary by a UK parent – and less so in the second, because of its move to greater financial control as it went global (Ahrens, op. cit.).

2.3 The concept of cost in Germany

2.3.1 Imputed costs

Costing statements will frequently show imputed costs such as replacement cost depreciation, provisions for warranties, the opportunity cost of equity or even an imputed wage for an owner-manager (Christenson and Wagenhofer, 1997; Busse von Colbe, 1996; Scherrer 1996; Schneider, 1995; Coenenberg and Schoenfeld, 1990). This feature was not immediately recognised by UKP in GS. Christenson and Wagenhofer (op. cit.) note that Siemens has recently moved away from this basis, as has GS under UK influence.

2.3.2 Costing rules for goods sold to the state

Rules developed under the Third Reich set a uniform procedure for pricing goods sold to the state, including replacement cost depreciation and interest on assets, and they continue today (Busse von Colbe, 1996; Coenenberg and Schoenfeld, 1990).

2.3.3 Costing systems

Scherrer (1996) provides evidence on costing systems and finds that, although the theoretical literature is very strong on marginal standard costing, the most common method in practice is based on full costing (see Table 2.2).

Scherrer comments: 'The widespread use of full costing using actual costs is surprising. Many German enterprises use this despite its failure to provide information for operational decisions and cost control, both of which are among the most important purpose of management accounting.' It is worth noting that actual costing may provide a reasonable basis for setting future prices and controlling costs in a low inflation environment such as Germany.

Table 2.2: Summary of survey evidence on costing methods

Cost accounting system	Average percentage
Actual costing using full costs	53.6
Standard costing using full costs only	38.7
Standard costing using marginal costs only	12.5
Combined full and marginal standard costing	39.3
Contribution margin accounting	36.7
Activity based costing	3.2

Note: multiple choices were permitted in the surveys.
Source: Scherrer (1996).

Thus a UK parent acquiring a German subsidiary may find its new subsidiary using some unfamiliar costing procedures and will need to decide to what extent changes need to be implemented to ensure consistency across the group. The same sorts of arguments, of course, also apply to a German parent acquiring a UK subsidiary.

2.4 Culture

Cultural differences may present significant barriers to the successful implementation of an acquisition strategy. Indeed they may influence the strategy.

There is substantial literature on how business culture varies from country to country, springing largely from the work of Hofstede. Hofstede initially identified four cultural dimensions but later added a fifth. Staff of IBM from different countries were asked to score these dimensions which were then ranked and allocated a score between 0 and 100 (Hofstede, 1991). Hofstede's dimensions are:

◆ individualism v. collectivism – the extent to which individuals are expected to look after themselves compared to societies which protect individuals in return for total loyalty;
◆ large v. small power distance – acceptance of hierarchy by the less powerful;
◆ strong v. weak uncertainty avoidance – the extent to which people can cope with ambiguity and uncertainty;
◆ masculinity v. femininity – preference for achievement, heroism, assertiveness and material success as against the more feminine preference for relationships, modesty, caring for the weak and the quality of life;
◆ long-term orientation – an East-West contrast, placing a value on perseverance, thrift and respect for status.

The German and British scores and ranks on these dimensions are shown in Table 2.3.

Hofstede only shows significant differences between Germany and Britain on individualism, where Germans are more collective, and on uncertainty avoidance, where Germans are less tolerant of ambiguity and uncertainty. Potentially these differences could be quite influential in the design of management control systems, affecting such things as the nature of incentive arrangements, management style, attitudes

Table 2.3: German and British scores on Hofstede's cultural dimensions

Dimension	Germany Score	Rank	Great Britain Score	Rank
Individualism index	67	15/53	89	3/53
Power distance index	35	42=/53	35	42=/53
Masculinity index	66	9=/53	66	9=/53
Uncertainty avoidance index	65	29/53	35	47=/53
Long-term orientation index	31	14/23	25	18/23

Source: Hofstede (1991).

to risk and uncertainty, and the degree of decentralisation. The last might affect budgetary control arrangements and the precision applied to costing and other data preparation. Indeed the case studies show some interesting cultural differences which may be explained using Hofstede's framework.

However, there are limitations with Hofstede's research which include:

◆ being out of date – the research was conducted in the 1970s and 1980s;
◆ by controlling for firm and professional cultures we cannot rank the different cultures in terms of importance;
◆ sampling the employees of a US multinational may be unrepresentative;
◆ the whole scoring system is based on averages without an indication of the degree of spread around these meaning that we cannot determine the statistical significance of any differences;
◆ questionnaires tend to attract idealised answers, indicating how people feel things ought to be, but not necessarily how they are.

Trompenaars and Hampden-Turner (1997) put forward a different cultural model, based on relationships with people, attitudes to time and attitudes to the environment – characteristics that could potentially affect strategy and a management control system. It is not feasible to generalise much about Anglo-German differences from Trompenaars *et al.* (op. cit.), but it does illustrate one difference that visitors to Germany are soon aware of, the diffuse versus the specific dimension. It concerns the nature of personal relations at work. Germans are very formal and can address work colleagues of many years as Mr. or Dr.

and this formality extends to all aspects of life, so that Dr. Schmidt is Dr. Schmidt, wherever he is encountered. However, where Germans know each other well enough to address each other as 'Du' (the informal version of you) and to use first names, they will do so for all purposes. It follows that in cross-border firms, staff may have to learn to operate in two different modes, sometimes using first names in English, but using formal address in German. A UK company acquiring a German firm has to decide whether it wishes to impose Anglo-Saxon style informality, as some US firms do as a matter of policy. Issues such as these need to be addressed in deciding how to implement the acquisition strategy, since cultural differences can be significant barriers to the successful implementation of a merger strategy.

Cultural differences extend to the varying levels of influence of different stakeholder groups in the two countries. The Anglo-Saxon model places shareholders above all other stakeholder groups and this is recognised in law, as well as being clear to any observer of the behaviour and rhetoric of British and American companies. The German corporate entity is clearly rather different, most obviously in the way legal rights to information and involvement in decision making are given to the workers. The supervisory board (see 2.6 below) also provides a mechanism through which other stakeholder groups such as banks, regional governments, large shareholders, customers and suppliers, can be involved in governance. These arrangements reflect significant differences in the perceived rights of the various stakeholder groups, which have a significant impact on the way business is conducted. Although large German companies have, in recent years, espoused the language of shareholder value, it is not so clear as to what extent they have fundamentally changed their view of the relative importance of stakeholder groups. However, many companies have embraced US GAAP or IAS, started holding road shows for analysts and including share performance information in their annual reports.

These differences in stakeholder influence will undoubtedly affect any UK company which acquires a German subsidiary and vice versa. They are potentially important because they impact on how any added value is distributed. The normal Anglo-Saxon assumption is that all added value should accrue to shareholders and the net present value (NPV) approach to investment appraisal reflects that. However, where other stakeholder groups are influential, they may have claims on added value, reducing what is available to shareholders.

The contractual view of culture has something in common with the stakeholder approach. It is concerned with the network of contracts, both formal and informal, which make up a company. A company thus may have very formal contracts with its suppliers, but may have informal understandings with its workforce about how much labour flexibility it can expect. Business culture can thus be seen to be a result of these networks of contracts, which in Germany, both formally through law and informally through managerial practice, afford much greater rights to the workforce and its representatives. This may significantly compromise any strategy devised by a UK parent focused on adding value for shareholders and is thus very relevant in the context of these case studies.

2.5 Capital markets

2.5.1 Short-termism

The main issue is the controversial question of short-termism. Many claim that Anglo-Saxon style capital markets lead to an excessive concern with short-term performance at the expense of the longer-term well-being of the company. The main shareholding group in Germany is industrial and commercial companies (Charkham 1994), who often hold large stakes (Jenkinson and Ljungqvist, 1997), unlike UK financial institutions, which are well diversified and hold only small stakes in individual companies. These shareholders have long-term strategic motives for their investment, are likely to be loyal and friendly and are unlikely to be very concerned about financial reporting. They have supervisory board membership and, in theory, can deal with poor managerial performance through this board.

2.5.2 Financing

The Stock Exchange in Germany is much less important than it is in the UK. As at 31 December 1998, the UK had over 2400 listed companies, whereas Germany had only 700 (London Stock Exchange, 1999)[1]. Traditionally, banks in Germany have played a bigger role in providing finance for industry. Furthermore, it is estimated (Edwards and Fischer, 1994) that listed companies account for about 30 per cent of total turnover in the UK as compared to only about 10 per cent in Germany. Medium-sized companies (Mittelstand) are also economically more important in Germany.

[1]It is interesting to note that the pace of change in corporate Germany is so fast that by 31 December 1999, Germany had 1043 quoted companies, whereas London had 2292 (Deutsche Börse, 2000).

2.5.3 Voting rights

In Germany, banks hold about 10 per cent of shares (Charkham, 1994), but in practice wield much greater power, because they exercise proxy votes on behalf of many shareholders, who hold bearer shares lodged with the bank.

2.5.4 Pension funds

In Germany, the state is the main provider of pensions and company pensions are simply provided by making annual accruals. This means that the funding remains in the company and is available for use, whereas in the UK, pension contributions are invested outside the company in the stock market. This is important for an acquisition in Germany because of the liability attaching.

Collectively, all of the above have consequences for strategic acquisition (the hostile takeover of a public company is very unlikely, despite the recent example of Vodafone and Mannesmann), investment appraisal (in terms of the thresholds set) and who gets to see management accounting information.

2.6 Corporate governance

The main Anglo-German difference in the corporate governance area is the existence in Germany of two-tier boards (Foster, 1996). As well as a management board (Vorstand) in charge of day-to-day operations, there is also a supervisory board (Aufsichtsrat), made up of shareholder and worker representatives, whose role is to monitor the performance of the executives. It is common for various stakeholder groups such as banks, Land government (the Federal Republic of Germany consists of a number of Länder or regions), shareholders, major customers or suppliers, as well as trades unions and the workforce – to be represented on the supervisory board. The detailed legal requirements depend on the legal status and size of the company. There are also special rules for companies in the steel and coal industries (Montan Mitbestimmung, Montan Co-determination). The key differences are that worker representatives have a veto on the appointment of a labour director and the supervisory board has equal numbers of worker and shareholder representatives plus one neutral member. If a company has more than 2000 employees, the supervisory board will be made up of equal numbers of employee and shareholder representatives, although the chairman, who has a casting vote, is from the shareholders' side (Mitbestimmungsgestez 1976, Co-determination Law, 1976). The number of members depends on the size of the company. It is compulsory to have a labour director, although there is no workers' right of veto, as with coal and steel companies.

With smaller companies, including private companies (GmbH) with over 500 employees, employee representatives constitute only one-third of the supervisory board (Betriebsverfassungsgesetz 1952, Works Council Law, 1952). Thus even where a company is a 100 per cent subsidiary, it may still be required to have a supervisory board in order to allow the workers some say in governance. In an AG (stock corporation) the supervisory board formally appoints the executive board and fixes its remuneration (Edwards and Fischer, 1994). The supervisory board is not involved in day-to-day decision making, but may be required under the articles to approve certain decisions made by the executives. Supervisory board meetings may only take place three or four times per annum, so the involvement of members is rather less than might be expected of a British non-executive director (Charkham, 1994).

Questions have been raised as to how effective this mechanism is, since supervisory boards meet so infrequently and the existence of two-tier boards has not prevented corporate scandal and other problems arising. Nevertheless, any British company acquiring a German company may find itself to some extent with a supervisory board containing worker representatives and having access to internal management information. Conversely, a German company acquiring a UK subsidiary will find itself without such institutional arrangements for the representation of a wider range of stakeholder groups.

It must be realised that supervisory boards are an important part of the apparatus of co-determination (Mitbestimmung), but that the most important organ of co-determination is the works council (see 2.7 below).

2.7 Co-determination

A major difference between the UK and Germany lies in the legal rules, which require German companies to have works councils, if the employees so request, and to provide these with information and discuss certain workplace issues with them. Indeed, in some areas, things can only be done with the agreement of the works council. Thus UK firms acquiring German firms may find that the timescale for workplace changes is rather longer and that actions have to be explained and people persuaded before such actions as reducing the workforce can be agreed. The whole area is heavily regulated by the law and resort to special labour courts will arise when agreed solutions cannot be found. The case studies explore further what is involved in practice.

The Betriebsverfassungsgestz, 1952 (Works Council Law, 1952) requires all firms with over five employees to set up works councils, whose size depends upon the size of the workforce. Members are elected to it every four years and there are no outside members. The works council will liaise closely with the personnel department and will meet periodically with management. The employer bears all the costs of the works council and must allow paid time off work for its members in the course of their duties. Within a group each subsidiary will have its own works council; in addition, there will be a group works council.

Works councils have various rights:

◆ to agree to certain actions, e.g. changes to working hours, introduction of new technology, pension administration, premium rates and performance related remuneration, training, Social Plan (establishing a fund for redundancies);
◆ to consultation and information, e.g. the works council's economic committee (formed where there are more than 100 employees) has wide rights to information on the financial situation of the company, accident prevention, personnel planning;
◆ veto some decisions, e.g. dismissal, redeployment, recruitment (Lane, 1989).

There are also significant differences in labour law, which offer employees rather greater protection than is found is less-regulated Anglo-Saxon labour markets. High *de facto* employment security and strong works council involvement forces managers to engage in more careful and long-term manpower planning (Lane, 1989). However, there is more scope for flexibility within the firm, partly because trade unions are not organised along craft lines. Flexibility about working hours is not uncommon with total hours for the year being fixed, but flexibility within this framework, as we have seen

BMW impose on its former UK subsidiary, Rover. National pay agreements are binding, but are implemented locally in consultation with the works council, which will determine a range of conditions of service. However, works councils have obvious incentives to encourage investment and to secure the long-term success of the firm, even if this occasionally involves job losses in the short run.

These differences in the role of labour in the running of the company have a significant potential to impact on strategy. For instance, a strategy which attempts to substitute capital for labour may take longer to implement in Germany and may involve the disclosure of information UK managers would usually keep confidential. Co-determination may also affect the type of information required from a management control system, as well as how widely that information is disseminated.

2.8 German managers, organisational structure and rewards

2.8.1 Managers

In Germany, engineering dominates finance with most managers being technical specialists rather than generalists and with boardrooms dominated by managers from a production background (Lane, 1989). There is no general management education in Germany and no MBA courses or their equivalent. German managers are generally better educationally qualified than UK managers in the sense that most will be graduates and quite a few will have doctorates. They start their careers later because German higher education takes longer, and may have fewer changes of employer during their careers (Warner and Campbell, 1997). They have to operate in a different environment, where consultation with the representatives of the workforce over a wide range of issues is a fact of life.

2.8.2 Organisational structure

Hierarchies in German firms tend also to be flatter, because supervisory grade staff will have received better vocational training and can thus have more tasks delegated to them. These differences may have considerable implications for a UK company trying to impose an organisational structure (as part of the management control system) upon an acquisition.

2.8.3 Rewards

There are some differences in incentive schemes. For legal reasons, stock options have been very rare, but the position is slowly changing. Research has found German managers' bonuses to be linked to rather broader criteria, including personal targets, whereas UK managers' performance-related elements have been more tightly linked to pure profitability (Coates, Davis and Stacey, 1995). This is not surprising, given differences in stakeholder influence and the determination of accounting profit – income smoothing and conservatism render reported profit levels a less reliable indicator of performance. The proportion of pay at risk does not differ significantly between the two countries, perhaps surprising in the light of Hofstede's work on attitudes to uncertainty. This may well change as large firms employ an increasingly cosmopolitan workforce and as German firms become more engaged in the Anglo-Saxon world. How multinational firms reconcile these different approaches to incentive arrangements is clearly an important issue in cross-border acquisitions, which, if handled badly, could impact negatively on the success of the acquisition.

Literature Review –
the Acquisitions Process

There is extensive finance, economics and management literature relating to acquisitions. The finance literature examines the effect on bidder and target shareholders' returns at the announcement date – impact returns – and the returns to the acquirer over the long term. The evidence is compelling: takeovers and mergers do not add value for the acquiring firm. The economics literature confirms the finance evidence but also looks at the welfare aspects of monopoly and economies of scale. The management literature focuses on managing foreign acquisitions but does not concentrate on accounting issues. This literature is also concerned with guarding against under-performance.

Similar results are to be found in professional survey research. Such research consistently shows that about half of all acquisitions fail to achieve the financial targets set at the time the acquisition was made (e.g. Coopers & Lybrand, 1993; Kitching, 1967).

What we have is that the benefits foreseen at the time of acquisition, and used to justify the acquisition decision, are not realised, or that there are costs unforeseen but subsequently realised, or both. There could be a number of reasons for this. These may not be separate or indeed independent but are listed below as if they were:

◆ The merger and acquisition (M&A) department has to justify its existence and may therefore be biased in its evaluation of potential takeover targets;
◆ The due diligence process is inadequate and failed to recognise future liabilities;
◆ Implementation may be flawed. Many authors suggest that problems arise in making acquisitions work, because they are planned from a strategic point of view based on the identification of potential synergies, without adequate consideration being given to how these synergies will be realised (Goold and Campbell, 1998; David and Singh, 1994).
◆ The amount of investment in managerial time is inadequate or underestimated, or the expertise is unavailable (Kitching op. cit.; Grundy op. cit.). Indeed a company should not make an acquisition where it lacks the resources to implement it, unless the target's incumbent management is of such quality that it can be left to get on with things with minimal intervention (Kitching op. cit.). These problems will be more difficult to resolve in the context of a cross-border acquisition;

◆ Business cultures do vary from country to country and the lack of good communication between the two parties may lead to failure. Culture will include differences in 'how you practise business' as well as priorities given to different stakeholder relationships (David and Singh, 1994). The acquirer's knowledge of the culture, customs, institutions and markets of the country in which the acquired company is located are likely to be deficient, making the parent more dependent on the existing management team (Bengtsson, 1992). Conversely, the managers and staff of the acquired company face greater uncertainty than in a domestic acquisition because they are not familiar with the managerial behaviour and corporate custom of the acquirer. Paramount is the need for a shared vision;

◆ Bad integration processes can destroy value (Grundy, 1998) and may be a major reason why so many mergers fail (Coopers & Lybrand, 1993; Kitching, 1967). Bad integration (Grundy op. cit.) can result from inadequate planning, abrupt changes in management style leading to low morale, the loss of key staff or the unnecessary imposition of new ways of doing things. Furthermore, the speed of integration needs to be considered. Is it better to introduce change slowly and gradually or to go for big bang change? According to Bengtsson (1992) changes are better made sooner than later. Staff expect changes to follow an acquisition and making the changes as quickly as possible minimises uncertainty.

Of these ideas, integration requires further consideration. The degree and type of integration of an acquired company depends upon the strategy for the acquisition and the control style of the parent. This literature presupposes that integration is a must for all acquisitions – but is this the case? Traditionally, mergers and acquisitions are classified as vertical, horizontal and conglomerate (where there is no industrial connection between the companies in the group). Clearly, conglomerate acquisitions require strong financial controls, but need little other integration beyond financial systems. In contrast, a vertical acquisition requires much greater integration in areas such as production and marketing. A horizontal acquisition may be integrated or not – it will depend upon managerial style.

The degree of integration of an acquired company also depends on the control style of the parent. Some groups will regard the business as geocentric (Perlmutter, 1969) or with a world orientation, seeking the group's best people to solve problems anywhere in the world. This approach requires excellent communication and time invested in reaching consensus. Such a group will have world-wide as well as local objectives. It will also need to have systems and incentives in place to encourage this sort of behaviour. Perlmutter (op. cit.) also outlines two other models, ethnocentric (home-country oriented) and polycentric (host-country oriented). In the former, the nationality of the parent defines the nationality of the group around the world and foreign subsidiaries exist to carry out work for the parent. In the polycentric group, we should expect to find a loosely connected group with quasi-independent subsidiaries held together by financial controls and with a great deal of weight given to local environmental factors. It is clear, however, that control style cannot be considered independently of the strategic objectives of the acquisition.

It was noted above that these reasons are not independent – an example of this would be the due diligence process covering not only strategic fit, but also organisational and cultural fit (David and Singh, 1994). For example, matching control and compensation systems can be more complex than companies imagine (Op. cit.). Compensation schemes have to take account of local conditions in order to recruit staff, whilst also taking account of group policies and the need for consistency.

What is largely missing from this literature is the role of the management accountant in evaluating the acquisition strategy and implementing the management control system. The case studies, therefore, seek to focus upon management accounting with a framework that looks at the organisation structure and responsibility centres, performance measurement and incentives.

It is being strongly argued that the management accountant has a very important role to play in identifying, clarifying, communicating and delivering a successful acquisition.

The Research Framework

The basic analytical model underlying the two cases is shown in Figure 4.1.

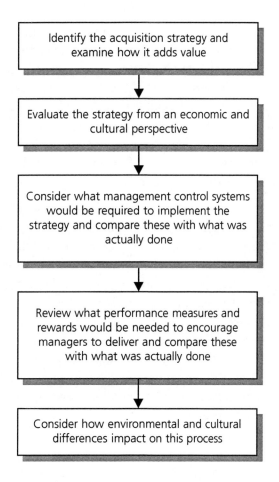

Figure 4.1 The analytical model of acquisition and management control

This framework of analysis begins with identifying the acquisition strategy and whether it has the potential to add value. It is essential that management accountants are involved and understand the strategic intent. Only then can they consider what type of management control system (MCS) is required in order to extract this value. It may be that there is added value, but without the control system in place the value could be acquired by others. The framework for the MCS will involve establishing an organisational structure with decision-making authority – responsibility centres in management accounting terms – deciding on performance measures – not necessarily only financial –

and the reward structure to create the appropriate incentives. This can then be compared with what actually happened and lessons can then be learnt.

Data were collected primarily through structured interviews with managers and accountants in both the parent companies and the subsidiaries. Wherever feasible, interviewees were identified in advance of the visit and given notice of the areas to be covered. Most interviews were tape-recorded and transcribed, with the interviewee given the opportunity to correct the transcript. The authors interviewed both accounting staff and managers to gather information to complete the analytical framework. The staff, their role and background in the acquisition is shown in Appendix 3.

In both cases, the parent was visited before the subsidiary, so that the visit to the subsidiary would be informed by knowledge of the rationale for the acquisition and of the parent's view of the problems which had arisen. Interview information was supplemented by accounting reports and other company information. Furthermore, information on the nature of the companies' businesses was collected and factory tours undertaken to fully understand the processes involved. This two-way investigation for each case study and the accumulation of confirmatory written evidence ensured construct validity (providing a chain of evidence), internal validity and a reliable outcome. Repeating the methodology on another case provided external validity of the approach.

Case Study One –
UK Parent and
German Subsidiary

5.1 Background information on the companies and the strategic motivation for the acquisition

5.1.1 Brief history of developments

UKP is a large quoted British manufacturing company. GS was acquired in 1991 from a German parent company, which was selling off some of its subsidiaries. At acquisition, GS had four directors (Geschäftsführer) – for production (also the Managing Director (MD)), sales, personnel and finance – and these were left in place. The company also had over 2000 employees. Since acquisition, GS has struggled to make profits and has restructured, reducing the workforce to about 1000, closing down some small subsidiaries and reducing the four directors to two. Of these two, the director responsible for personnel and finance remains from the time of the acquisition, while the other was brought in from elsewhere in the group. The latter is German: he is MD and has sales responsibility across the whole of the division. There is a new finance controller, who is formally responsible to the Personnel Director, but on day-to-day matters deals direct with the UK Divisional Controller, and also a new head of financial reporting under GS's controller. These personnel changes were made several years after the acquisition, but have been key in allowing UKP to achieve control and in integrating GS into the group.

5.1.2 Motives for the acquisition

There were *four* main motives in the acquisition with vertical economies seen as the most important:

◆ **Diversification** – diversify away from a predominantly British base and the exposure to the UK's economic cycle;
◆ **Market power in the product range** – remove a competitor and make UKP a much larger world player within this specialist area;
◆ **Efficiency gains** – improve upon the managerial ability at GS;
◆ **Economies from vertical integration** – some companies within the parent group had an option to supply surplus intermediate stock to GS for further processing.

Although the acquisition was not material in terms of the group as a whole, it was material in terms of the specialist area, where GS was larger than the group's UK specialist businesses, and the acquisition made UKP a much larger global player. For tax reasons, GS was established as a limited partnership (Gesellschaft mit beschränkter Haftung und Co., GmbH & Co.) in which the unlimited partner is a limited liability company. This legal structure is relatively common in Germany, although unknown in the UK.

5.1.3 Comparison of UKP's and GS's businesses

Before it is possible to evaluate the strategy we need to say more about the activities of UKP and GS:

◆ UKP is basically a commodity supplier, interested in bulk production of a limited product range. UKP holds low stocks and is set up to deliver finished goods to customers (largely at wholesale level) as soon as they have been produced;
◆ GS has an extensive product range and makes specialist items, many bespoke and often involving a high degree of finishing. Many of the orders are small:
  – There are high set-up times with lengthy changeover and trial times, so production lot size is very important in terms of its impact on costs. For some production lines at GS, available time may only be about 50 per cent of capacity;
  – Many customers provide specialist tools for producing their orders;
  – GS receives indicative orders from final customers against which it produces. Customers collect finished goods at their convenience, resulting in GS holding very high levels of stock. This is a service which its customers expect. GS sells mainly in the German market, but exports to the US and the Far East.

5.2 Analysis of the acquisition strategy

Each motive is now considered in turn.

5.2.1 Diversification

The question is: can UKP add value – to shareholders – by diversifying away from a predominantly UK market by acquiring GS with its predominantly German market? It is important to note that the UK and German activities have not been on the same economic cycle so there is some risk reduction potential. However, the standard argument in the finance literature is that this potential for risk reduction cannot be value adding to shareholders. Shareholders can themselves easily hold a portfolio of UK and German stocks and achieve for themselves any risk reduction benefits. More recently, diversification has been interpreted in the literature in terms of achieving synergy benefits through joining two activities. This interpretation is not relevant here and will be considered under vertical integration (see 5.2.4). From a managerial perspective, of course, things may look quite different, as managers cannot diversify risk in the way that investors can.

5.2.2 Removal of a competitor

The industry in which UKP and GS operate is global with many competitors of varying sizes. This acquisition was not material in altering the concentration and hence the level of competition in the industry. As a result, the acquisition could not have generated any gains from additional market power. The lack of any regulatory interest in the merger by the UK, German or EU competition authorities is strong evidence that no monopoly gain would be forthcoming.

5.2.3 Efficiency gains

As in all combinations there are opportunities for efficiency gains. One of the standard arguments for gains from takeovers and mergers is that the present management of a business is not achieving the maximum output from a given set of inputs. A new management could impose a new regime and extract extra value from such efficiencies for the benefit of shareholders. While there is little evidence that efficient firms acquire inefficient firms there remains an opportunity for UKP to achieve some efficiency in GS.

5.2.4 Vertical integration

This dimension constitutes the very rationale developed by the M&A department at UKP. Economies of vertical integration occur when the payoffs to vertically separated firms are less than the payoff to an integrated firm. Standard arguments for vertical integration are:

◆ **Security of supply:** for inputs critical to continuity of production, having them sourced internally reduces risks of quality and hold-ups;

- **Investment externalities:** if a large investment by a firm in a vertical chain can only pay off if there is a long-term agreement with the firm down the chain then one way of guaranteeing the payoff is to acquire the downstream firm;

- **Physical contiguity of processes:** an integrated production process can often produce efficiencies as well as reduced stock-holding costs;

- **Market power:** there may be an opportunity to exploit monopoly power by increasing barriers to entry – for example, by cross-subsidising products.

None of these arguments apply here. The intermediate product is homogeneous, almost a commodity product, and the industry has low entry barriers with significant economies of scale in production and an absence of specific investments by buyer and seller for standard products. Market procurement should be the best strategy.

However, the rationale for vertical integration, in this case, was based on the international nature of the acquisition and foreign exchange (FX) fluctuation between the UK and Germany. Specifically, at one exchange rate (say 2.50DM/£) it would be profitable to sell from UKP to GS while at another (say 3.00DM/£) it would not. What we have is a *real investment option* – the acquisition would pay off when the option 'was in the money'.

At the time the strategy was being developed, some modelling of exchange rate movements did take place. As Appendix 2 shows, the exchange rate has been particularly volatile over the period, with the pound (using quarterly data) falling as low as DM2.206 and rising as high as DM3.098 during the 1991–98 period. Clearly, the real option was 'in the money' suggesting that the strategy could work.

However, there are some issues:

- The strategy ignores other FX movements. This is an international business with an opportunity for GS to source from anywhere in the world. Even if the DM/£ exchange rate looks to be 'in the money' there may be other better deals on offer[2].;

- It assumes that UK prices were fixed with respect to the DM/£ FX rate;

- Transport costs: the intermediate product is a bulk commodity and therefore costly to transport from the UK to Germany. But GS was incurring transport costs with its existing supply arrangements and it is unlikely that the net incremental transport costs are greater than the change in the FX rate;

◆ Commodity price volatility: the intermediate product price was subject to price volatility. The effect of this volatility has meant that contracts for supply which locked in the FX gain could be more expensive than buying in the international market at the new lower spot price;

◆ Cultural aspects of the strategy: the strategy assumes that contracts with German suppliers of the intermediate good can be switched on and off easily and quickly. It is common for German contracts to be 'relational', involving long-term contracts. This would make it impossible to take advantage of short-term volatility in the exchange rate. GS's managers did not feel that they could switch their German suppliers on and off in the way that would have been required.

5.2.5 Conclusion on strategy evaluation

Of the four elements only two – vertical integration and efficiency – have any potential, but a potential that looks slight. It is perhaps no surprise to learn that, in practice, GS has never been a significant outlet for surplus UK stock and that the acquisition strategy has never been fulfilled.

5.3 UKP's management control system and implementing the strategy

To realise the potential gain UKP would have needed to set up an appropriate management control system. Before looking at what actually happened, we need to consider what management control system

---

[2]There is a further economic issue as to whether the strategy would work. When the FX rate is favourable, what is the level of aggregate demand in the German economy? Recall that it was not part of the strategy to change the marketing strategy of GS. If, for example, the option is 'in the money' when demand for the finished good is low there would be no need to exercise the option. Now, it could be argued that with prices fixed in the short term, a monetary expansion under flexible FX rates and capital mobility leads to a depreciation of the currency and an increased gross domestic product (GDP). In these circumstances, the strategy would work – when the FX rate is favourable there is increased aggregate demand in the economy.

might have helped deliver the strategy of vertical integration and efficiency. We then go on to consider incentive arrangements to deliver each strategy.

5.3.1 Vertical integration

In general, there are two types of solution, either decentralised or centralised. Thus whilst it is possible to go for a centralist solution, it is probably more common to allow greater autonomy and place more reliance on incentive mechanisms and monitoring.

A decentralised approach

The buy/sell decision is devolved and appropriate performance measures and incentives are used to ensure the strategy is delivered. If the standard profit centre model had been applied to the new subsidiary, it would have been controlled through the annual budget-setting cycle and monthly reporting. In particular, the focus on profit (as a performance measure) and a managerial incentive (based on the attainment of a profit target), together with a system of flexible budgeting would have identified the gains from vertical integration and efficiency. GS's profit would have been boosted by transfers of surplus intermediate product from the UK if the transfer price was – FX adjusted – in the money[3].

Flexing the budget of GS for FX values would serve as both a planning and co-ordinating tool, as well as identifying the differential performance effects of vertical integration and efficiency on the control side. In such a flexible budget, the budget targets would be a function of the FX rate. Different budgets would be calculated for each FX rate, reflecting whether or not the real option was to be exercised. Flexing, in this context, is not about controllability, which is the usual case where flexing is for volume levels, for clearly the managers of GS cannot control the FX rate, but about identifying the specific source of any gains. Such an approach would have put very strong pressure on GS's managers to exercise the real option when it was in the money, as without doing so they would not be able to meet their budget targets.

---

[3] There is, however, an issue for UKP's UK subsidiaries which supply the intermediate product in that their reported profits might have been higher producing the product for stock rather than selling it to GS at marginal cost plus contribution.

Of course, flexing a budget for GS would have been redundant if UKP had set the FX rate in the transfer price in DM at some rate different from the market rate so as to force the strategy (and eliminate any exchange risk for GS) and guarantee GS higher profits. However, doing this would not identify the value of any FX option and hence the value of vertical integration.

Simons' (1990) idea of management control systems focusing on strategic uncertainties may be relevant here. UKP's strategy for the acquisition of GS depends critically upon the DM/£ exchange rate. Therefore, the management control systems used by top management to implement strategy should reflect this. Furthermore, Simons (op. cit.) suggests that managers lack time and should use interactive management control in those areas where they wish to signal to subordinates the importance of a particular area. Top managers should get involved in monitoring those strategic uncertainties which are critical to achieving the firm's goals.

A centralised approach

An alternative solution would be to take the decision rights both from UKP's UK subsidiaries supplying the intermediate product and from GS by setting up a 'trading unit' to execute transfers when exchange rate conditions were right. The unit itself could have operated as a cost centre, whose performance could have been assessed in non-financial terms by the volume of transfers made, or as a profit centre extracting some of the arbitrage opportunity for itself, with its performance evaluated on sales margin. It could, furthermore, have bought in sterling and sold in deutschmarks, leaving the UK subsidiaries and GS to be evaluated solely in local currency terms.

5.3.2 Efficiency

Consideration also needs to be given to the question as to how the efficiency gains envisaged by UKP at the time of acquisition might be delivered through the management control system. It would be critical that GS's budgetary control system focused on the performance measures, both financial and non-financial, which are critical to achieving greater efficiency. Efficiency gains require greater output from given inputs, and the most obvious way of achieving this at GS is through higher utilisation levels[4]. Thus, such measures as set-up and changeover times, or overall utilisation measures, may have been suitable indicators. Average cost might also be used, as this should fall as utilisation improves. As we know, these performance measures need to meet two criteria – they should be capable of objective measurement and correlate with added value to the business. Here these examples meet the first criteria but may not meet the second. Some products with high set-up costs may carry a large enough price premium to add value, despite the inefficiencies in their production, and average cost may not be a guide to added value when what we want is incremental cost compared with incremental revenue.

5.3.3 Incentive arrangements to deliver the strategy

Incentive arrangements are an important element in delivering strategy, especially where a high level of autonomy is granted to the newly acquired subsidiary. Performance measures and incentives need to be put in place to encourage managers to deliver the strategy. In transnational groups, there is the further problem that incentive packages may differ from country to country and the group has to decide whether to impose a world-wide scheme and what allowances to make for local differences.

Incentives and vertical integration

The vertical integration strategy based on FX rates could have been reinforced through suitable incentive arrangements. When the option is 'in the money' profits should have increased at GS. Thus, any profit-related incentives should have encouraged GS's managers to buy surplus UK intermediate product. As was noted earlier, this would depend on the ability and willingness of GS's managers to switch on and off their contracts with German suppliers.

Incentives and efficiency

The other strand to the strategy was to improve efficiency. In the case of GS, the main way to achieve this is through higher utilisation levels, which could easily be built into a bonus arrangement.

---

[4]Utilisation improvement is inevitably linked to investment. One of the main motives for buying up-to-date plant is that set-up times can be vastly reduced by improved technology. However, as is discussed later, UKP's system of capital expenditure controls inhibited GS's ability to improve utilisation in this way.

As a general point, one would expect the imposition of a budgetary control package to be a key feature of post-acquisition strategy in any acquisition, with the subsidiary being brought rapidly into the group's monthly budgetary control timetable and required to produce reports in English and in a standard group format.

5.4 Review of the actual management control system

UKP perceives that GS has been a considerable problem and that a large part of this problem lies in the accounting area. It has taken UKP years to get GS's accounting systems onto the sort of basis that it wants and producing the information required in a timely manner, and even now concerns about excessive complexity and the timing of the recognition of variances remain.

To analyse what has actually happened the following framework is adopted. The focus is upon:

- ◆ the structure of the organisation as a result of the acquisition;
- ◆ the style of budgetary control;
- ◆ costing systems;
- ◆ the performance measures set down for the acquired unit;
- ◆ the incentive rewards to motivate staff;
- ◆ information systems;
- ◆ capital expenditure approval.

Cultural differences are then also considered.

5.4.1 The structure of the organisation – the responsibility centres

UKP has organised its businesses into 12 divisions each with its own MD and Finance Controller. In turn, each division is part of four portfolios, each the responsibility of a main board director. The division to which GS belongs was created at the time of the acquisition and is relatively small within UKP. However, GS is the largest subsidiary company in its division and is considerably larger than the UK members of the division. Thus, GS reports initially to its division in the UK, which in its turn reports to a main board director, who also has his own finance director.

In the division containing GS there are overlaps in responsibilities and product ranges, creating opportunities for conflicts of interest. For example, the Managing Director of GS has commercial responsibility for the whole division and therefore must choose where to put particular orders within the division. The lack of rationalisation of the production process was the result of the need for specialist tools owned by particular customers and the fact that some German customers prefer to buy from German suppliers. However, recent restructuring in the UK part of the division has prioritised the rationalisation of production.

5.4.2 The style of budgetary control

Within the group it is normal for subsidiaries to operate as profit centres with the usual mechanisms of annual budget setting and monthly monitoring plus procedures for agreeing capital expenditure. Such an approach is common in Germany too, so UKP adopted its normal decentralised solution with GS. However, there were problems as follows.

Implementation

GS was given considerable autonomy because UKP lacked the managerial resource to implement a strategy of change and integration – UK staff attended GS approximately two days per month and no GS staff visited the UK. UKP lacked German speakers and had only three staff at divisional level so could not spare anyone to manage the process full time. It also appears that promises were made to incumbent staff about how little change there would be after the acquisition, in order to calm the fears of the managers and the workforce.

Budgetary reporting

Reporting problems ranked high in UKP's list of problems with GS. Reports were long, complicated and in German, and did not contain all the information UKP wanted or felt was important. They were also, for many years, reporting one month in arrears and using a different period end from the rest of the group. Thus it cannot be said that UKP was successful in imposing an appropriate system of financial controls and it took many years, in some cases, to sort out fairly basic reporting requirements. (For a complete exposition see Appendix 4.)

Budget formulation

Although restrictive German labour practices and the legal requirement to consult the works council about a wide range of issues might
be expected to affect the planning timescale of German companies,
there was no evidence from this case of differences in planning horizon. The usual situation in both UKP and GS was to have a detailed
annual budget for the next year and rather vaguer plans for the following two years.

GAAP issues

There are some GAAP differences which were not understood by UKP
and which affect performance measurement.

◆ **Pension liabilities:**
  – This is a major GAAP difference;
  – There are differences in the calculation of the liability. In
    Germany, it is based upon years of *actual* service, whereas in
    the UK it is based on *expected* years of service;
  – There is a significant difference in the way the liability is
    funded. German companies simply accrue their company pen-
    sion liabilities, keeping the funds within the company and
    available for use. In comparison, the British use a funded pen-
    sion scheme quite separate from the company itself.
  – The main board of UKP did not immediately understand this
    difference; for they feared that they had a huge pensions lia-
    bility and no assets. This suggests a failure in the due dili-
    gence process;
◆ **Stock valuation:**
  – In line with German management accounting practice, stock
    valuations included current cost depreciation and interest for
    internal reporting purposes, although such approaches were
    not allowed for financial reporting purposes;
  – When UKP ended these German practices there was concern
    that sales personnel, in preparing quotations, would not
    understand the need to earn a bigger margin, when the inter-
    est element (a proxy cost of capital charge) was removed from
    stock valuation;

◆ **Fixed assets – (festwert = fixed value)**

- German GAAP allows minor fixed assets to be shown at a fixed value, with replacements written off in the year of purchase, but subject to periodic inventory. If the inventory shows that the value is more than 10 per cent away from the fixed value, then adjustments to the Festwert have to be made through the P&L account;

- The aim is to simplify the accounting of inventory and minor fixed assets which are immaterial in the context of the company. It should be remembered that German rules require the capitalisation of assets costing over DM800 (approximately £300), so the need for such a rule can be appreciated;

- UK companies have greater freedom to set their own threshold for capitalisation. In the case of UKP it is £5000;

- The method is less used now than it was because with IT systems it is much easier to keep accurate records of inventory and fixed assets.

However, a major difference arose with costing systems, considered next.

5.4.3 Costing systems

Cost objectives

For UKP, product cost was the main objective. For GS, it was departmental costs.

Actual v. standard

UKP operated a standard costing system. In contrast, GS operated a modified actual costing system where direct costs were recorded at actual quantity and price, while indirect costs were at budgeted indirect rate at actual quantity.

UKP regarded the GS approach as unsatisfactory since it could not produce product variances. UKP proceeded to introduce a standard costing system where all transfers within GS were done at standard cost. UKP has not insisted that any particular detailed method be used to calculate costs but it requires certain types of variance to be calculated. Within this framework GS is allowed considerable latitude.

Cost allocation

UKP staff regarded GS's system as being unnecessarily complicated. GS had over 500 cost centres whereas some of UKP's UK plants in the division had 10. Whilst this partly reflects a difference in the complexity of the business, it does also reflect a different attitude to accounting. Furthermore, within each cost centre there could be more than 1 cost driver. This has now been simplified, so that under the recently introduced SAP R/3 there will be only 150 cost centres and only 1 cost driver for each.

Service cost allocation

GS used reciprocal cost allocation whereas UKP preferred the direct method. UKP's staff regarded such reciprocal charging as unnecessary and wasteful of administrative resource for no real benefit. The head of management accounting at GS, however, regarded the reciprocal charging (done on the basis of actual services rendered, not just an allocation) as reflecting reality and incentives – in particular, it made service cost managers more careful about how they used these resources. The trade-off of correctness against simplicity lies at the crux of this cultural clash.

Costing set-up and breakdowns

UKP bases its costing only on time actually spent processing. Thus set-up times, breakdowns, etc. are just part of the overhead and are averaged out across all products. This is simpler and treats the breakdown as a random event which is not product related. UKP accepts that this system with its constant lot size assumption is crude, but claims that allowance is made for different lot sizes in setting prices and in reading variances. It regards the standard costing system as a basic toolkit, rather than as a system for dealing with every eventuality.

In contrast at GS, breakdown costs were, in part, attributed to the product. GS staff claimed that their method differentiates breakdown costs into two categories:

◆ those that relate to the product and are charged to it;
◆ those that are random events and are spread out over all the production orders in that area for the month.

For instance, a breakdown due to a product-specific machine tool breaking would be treated as product specific, whereas a breakdown caused by an electrical problem would not.

Now that GS has a standard costing system in place, these differences just affect the variances, rather than the cost of stock, which once finished is valued at standard cost. GS also claims that it is right for it not just to average out set-up times across all products, as UK division members do, because these vary enormously from product to product, and to average them out would lose important information. In reality, GS has a system based on activity-based costing (ABC), in which specific cost drivers are used to attribute costs other than central overhead which is still apportioned as a percentage of conversion costs.

Variances

Staff at UKP are now satisfied at long last that GS produces variance statements in the right way, although it has taken years to reach this point. However, concern remains that the variances shown do not tie in with the physical figures. GS's accounts staff admit that there is a problem, because the present system only shows a variance when an order is completed and that might be some months after the production process. A concomitant of this is that work-in-progress is shown at actual cost and only converted to standard cost on completion, at which point the variances are struck and charged to the P&L account. This appears to reflect German GAAP's treatment of long-term contracts, where profit is only recognised on completion. With the installation of SAP R/3, it will be possible to improve the situation by splitting an order into a number of sub-orders and calculating variances after the completion of each stage. Nevertheless, the basic philosophy that a variance can only be struck on completion remains.

5.4.4 Performance measures

The key performance indicators across the whole division are now actual performance v. standard, flexed according to the actual mix, availability and speed of working, which together form the composite efficiency measure called the yield. The Head of Management Accounting now regards the introduction of standard costing as a step forward with better information and responsibility for their variances.

She also points out that when she first started work at GS over 20 years ago, calculations were done manually, and a system of such complexity could not then have been implemented.

5.4.5 Incentives

UKP imposed a division-wide incentive scheme for all senior managers based upon:

◆ profitability as against budget for the subsidiary;
◆ stock levels in the subsidiary;
◆ efficiency as measured by performance against standard taking account of availability and speed of working.

At GS this covers the top twenty managers. The bonus is paid quarterly and can be up to 18 per cent of salary. Because budget targets are regarded as hard to meet, some bonus may still be paid even if the target is not met. There are plans to add personal targets.

The following points regarding incentives should be noted:

◆ It is clear that business and cultural differences are not important. However, stock levels in the incentive arrangements reflect UKP's desire to keep stocks low. Its stock turnover is 12x p.a. compared to 5-6x p.a. at GS. The different relationships GS has with its customers and the need to manufacture in economic lot sizes is recognised by UKP in that GS has a much lower stock turnover target to trigger the bonus;
◆ Profitability should have encouraged the purchase of surplus intermediate product from the UK when the option was 'in the money', but this might not have been as effective as rewards tied directly to the quantity of transfers;
◆ The utilisation element should have provided an incentive to improve efficiency but, as explained below, capital expenditure procedures and limits reduced the effect;
◆ Senior management incentives within the division do not perfectly reflect responsibilities. The Division Finance Controller's bonus is linked to one UK plant's performance, whereas the Managing Director of GS, who has overall commercial responsibility, has a bonus linked to the performance of GS only;
◆ The Divisional Managing Director has a bonus based on the performance of the division (viz. profits, cash and working capital before translation effects) and of the group.

GS is moving its workforce bonus scheme onto a group basis, so that everyone in the group gets the same bonus. This deal has met some resistance from the works council, but is gradually being implemented. This decision was made in Germany and does not reflect any UKP imposition.

5.4.6 Information systems

Accounting software

The underlying question is whether parent and subsidiary need to use the same accounting software. A common package would facilitate a common management control framework, but in a cross-border acquisition is commonality necessary given that there may be problems relating to language? Of course a multi-lingual package solves the problem.

UKP's tailor-made accounting software, although not common throughout the group, could not be transferred to GS – it was in English, it was old and in need of replacement, and it was poorly documented. GS's own tailor-made software suffered from the same problems. As a consequence of the acquisition it changed to SAP R/2, converting more recently to SAP R/3. UKP has now installed SAP R/3.

Communications software

Communications software has also been a problem, with GS using Microsoft™ and UKP Lotus SmartSuite™. The ability to transfer data easily and avoid rekeying is essential. Having a common interface saved a day's time at divisional level in producing the monthly figures, but this was only achieved five years after the initial acquisition. The UK division would have preferred Microsoft but was constrained by group policy.

5.4.7 Capital expenditure approval

Most subsidiaries are set up as profit centres and not investment centres because the parent wants to retain control over decisions which can have important strategic consequences.

In UKP, a capital plan for two years ahead is agreed each January as part of the budget-setting process. Each business puts in bids and the division passes these on to the next level in the hierarchy for approval or rejection. The success rate is only about 20 per cent. The Managing Director of the division can approve expenditure up to £100,000. The investment-approval process is common across the group with a standard pro-forma, where cash-flows are set out in real terms. At the time of interview, projects approved at divisional level required a two-year payback and a 40 per cent internal rate of return (IRR) in real terms, but these criteria reflected a short-term response to difficult conditions. The more usual criteria are 6-year payback and 20 per cent IRR. Projects not meeting these criteria can still be approved at a level one step higher than usual. Thus the main Board Director, with responsibility for the division, can approve projects under £100,000 not meeting the criteria. There is a post-completion review for all projects over £3 million and 10 per cent of projects approved at divisional level. However, it is clear that this process is not very probing.

There is one hurdle rate used across the whole group, without adjustment for risk or for different national costs of funds. Managers at GS argue that, as a downstream business, it has a lower risk than the commodity end of the group and that it can borrow more cheaply in Germany. These two arguments taken together should lead to a lower discount rate.

It is important to note that GS has a history of underinvestment under UKP (and its previous parent) with annual depreciation being greater than capital investment.

5.5 Culture: Anglo-German differences

It is recognised in the academic literature that different national cultures can explain the choice of international strategy and corporate management control system (MCS), and that the use of an inappropriate system can destroy value. There are many taxonomies but the most commonly cited reference is Hofstede (1991). (See section 2.4.) Hofstede initially identified four significant cultural dimensions of which there were differences between German and UK managers on the dimensions of uncertainty avoidance and collectivism–individualism. How useful is this framework for interpreting the evidence here? We divide the differences into management accounting and broader business and cultural differences.

5.5.1 Management accounting differences

Status

There is a clear difference in status for finance which is much more important in a UK company than in a German company. In contrast, engineering and commercial interests were dominant in Germany. As a consequence, accountants were reluctant to challenge engineers, even when their figures did not make sense. Thus, approval of capital expenditure proposals was more of a formality than a real scrutiny. It also suggests that non-financial criteria were more important.

Engagement

Accountants at UKP felt that GS's accountants were divorced from the rest of the business, being reluctant to go down to the shop floor, something UK management accountants do regularly.

Precision

UKP accountants also felt that their German counterparts tried to be unnecessarily precise and were reluctant to make estimates, even where UK accountants regarded this as normal and necessary to meet timetable constraints. For instance GS's accountants:

◆ Would not estimate monthly payroll costs in order to get their monthly budget reports in on time;
◆ Had large numbers of cost centres and insisted on reciprocal recharging between service cost centres, whereas UKP management accountants preferred simpler methods. GS employed a member of staff to read meters so as to make precise recharges of energy costs to departments.

Education

There was a difference in background and training between management accountants in UKP and GS. UKP accountants were members of CIMA and had learned their accounting through a professional qualification. At GS, the finance staff were university graduates in business economics and/or had undertaken an accounting apprenticeship.

Accounting

There were significant differences in accounting, some of which continue. For example:

- using replacement cost depreciation in stock costs;
- adding interest into stock costs;
- using calendar months rather than 4–5 week periods for budget reports;
- the calculation of the pension liability.

5.5.2 Broader business and cultural differences

Attitudes towards hierarchy

UK interviewees claim that the Germans are more hierarchical and that it is more difficult than in the UK to go straight to a more junior member of staff with a query. It is expected that you deal with the senior staff member, with the consequence that UK staff have little contact with GS staff below the top level.

Social formality

UK interviewees found Germans to be socially more formal, addressing colleagues as Herr or Frau, rather than using first names, although one interviewee thought that younger Germans were less formal and more prepared to accept Anglo-Saxon norms. Furthermore, GS staff had to learn to operate in two modes, being informal when talking English with UK staff, and more formal when speaking German (see section 2.4).

Contractual arrangements

- **Customers**: GS has a different relationship with its customers, to whom it offers a much greater degree of finishing as well as a stock-holding service. It would appear that the use of indicative orders and stock-holding is common in Germany. From the evidence here, it is difficult to conclude whether this difference is cultural or business-specific. We do know that relational contracting is well understood under UK law, suggesting that it is the latter.

◆ **Labour:** There are significant differences in labour market contracts between the UK and Germany. German companies have less flexibility in shedding labour and need to consult with their works council about such issues in a heavily regulated environment, in which resort to the labour courts is not uncommon. It seems no coincidence that the Geschäftsführer for Personnel is a lawyer by training. The cost of shedding labour is also likely to be higher and Social Plan payments have to be properly budgeted and taken into account in any capital investment proposal which substitutes capital for labour. However, internally there is greater flexibility in shifting staff from one area to another. GS has also negotiated an annual hours' contract with its employees and is in the process of installing a group bonus scheme. It does, furthermore, employ some workers on temporary contracts, who do not enjoy the usual employment rights, in this way coping to some extent with the rigidities of German labour market regulation. Hence, the risks to capital do vary somewhat between Germany and the UK. German managers may not be able to shed labour costs so easily, but may have greater internal flexibility, to some extent at least offsetting the problem of cutting labour costs.

Labour participation in decision making and control

There are two worker representatives on the supervisory board (the chairman and deputy chairman of the works council), which meets twice a year and is chaired by the Divisional Managing Director. The fact that GS is a 100 per cent owned subsidiary does not remove the need for this additional layer of corporate governance. The supervisory board receives detailed information about the macro environment, budget reports and other financial information, as well as reports on safety, environmental issues, personnel and capital expenditure plans. GS's works council has fifteen members. Its economic committee receives information on the economic and financial situation of the business. As well as formal meetings there is routine contact between the works council and the personnel department. UKP tends to regard the co-determination procedures as expensive and burdensome, but the Geschäftsführer for Personnel sees them as useful and facilitating co-operative working.

Of these Anglo-German differences only precision seems to be captured by the Hofstede analysis. Many of them are to do with institutional differences which can affect the strategic objectives – as in this case – and will influence the mode of operating a management control system. Perhaps a great deal can be explained by the different cost objectives meaning that German management accountants are not involved with pricing or investment decisions and instead are concerned with control rather than decision making.

5.6 Conclusions

1. The acquisition strategy of vertical integration of GS has not been a success. During the period 1992–7 the DM/£ FX rate appeared favourable but the strategy was not implemented. It is plausible that the strategy could not work for other reasons. Perhaps this explains why no real attempt was made to establish the management control system required to make it happen. A management control system could have been put in place through a combination of flexible budgeting (flexed on FX rates) and incentives, but was not. Instead, the focus of the control system was the new structure of a specialist division including GS and UK subsidiaries. This could be interpreted as the implicit abandonment of the strategy and a shift of emphasis towards some rationalisation of the specialist area and the search for efficiency gains.

2. The strategy of improved efficiency could have easily been achieved by introducing new technology to reduce set up times. However, the control system did not support this. Instead, capital expenditure restrictions made it very hard for GS to get approval for clear, value-enhancing projects.

3. The due diligence process should have paid more attention to management accounting systems and how control should have been implemented.

4. Change management was vital to making the acquisition work. There were two issues here. First, it appears that UKP gave undertakings to the workforce not to change things when it took over GS. Clearly these promises hindered UKP in making changes to control systems. This lesson was not learnt by UKP, notwithstanding it was clear from the literature and was recognised by both German and UK interviewees. Second, changing key personnel was vital to making the acquisition work and this should have been done much sooner. UKP installed a new MD with pre-

vious experience of UKP and a new controller. Thus, although management accounting issues were a major issue in integrating GS, the fundamental issue was nevertheless the 'management of change'.

5. It is clear that UKP did not invest sufficient managerial time in imposing the necessary managerial control systems. They did not have anyone ready and based their control on periodic visits. Moreover, there was a lack of momentum when the accountant engaged in the acquisition process was transferred to another activity. This failure to provide managerial time is a common argument for the failure of any takeover or merger, but in this case it appears to be rather simplistic. The lack of managerial time does not explain why UKP did not:

◆ Impose its requirements. Why did UKP not insist on reports being on time (they were for a long time one month in arrears), written in English and using UKP's periods? Clearly the business and cultural differences need to be understood and taken account of but they do not constitute serious barriers to installing suitable management control;

◆ Understand the characteristics of GS's accounting systems and methods;

◆ After the due diligence process, appreciate how different GS's business was from UKP's in terms of product range, complexity and end customer focus, and therefore how difficult this made it to impose a standard costing system.

6. UKP had worked with standard costing as a control technique and therefore imposed it on GS. In so doing, it took inadequate account of the different nature of GS's business, which was too complex to be well suited for standard costing. Thus the implementation of standard costing was long and difficult. This was exacerbated by the use of SAP R/2 without the corresponding production package and the lack of interfaces with other data sources – it appears that much of the data, in particular the standards, simply were incorrect. The installation of a computerised, standard costing system was a much bigger step than UKP realised.

7. The use of SAP R/2 at GS, while UKP used another system, shows that there is no great need for all group companies to share a com-

mon software package, provided that the reporting requirements are clearly stated. However, commonality in communications packages would have been cheap and valuable.

8. It is extraordinary that on the one hand UKP had delegated the choice of software to GS with its complex approach to German management accounting, whilst on the other hand, deploring what it felt to be excessive cost accounting.

9. Accounting issues played a major part in the case study, with UKP feeling that its most severe problems in managing GS were accounting-related. UKP invested too little in getting to know GS. It was slow to note the impact of accounting differences, such as the treatment of long-term work-in-progress and its impact on the timing of variance recognition, the complexity of GS's costing system in terms of the number of cost centres and cost drivers, and the use of reciprocal costing.

10. The case study does show differences in the role and status of management accountants and in attitudes to uncertainty avoidance and the reluctance to make estimates. There is some evidence here of a clash of management accounting cultures, with UK management accounting more ready to sacrifice perfection for simplicity, but also more engaged in the business, whereas GS's finance function appears to have been concerned with precision, but without being tied into decision making. It also shows the well-known differences between German and British labour markets. However, they do not appear to be significant. For example, the differences in labour markets appear to have no differential impact on the planning horizon and certainly do not impact upon a suitable management control system.

11. The incentive arrangements were imposed across countries regardless of national cultural differences and business practice. For example, the collectivism–individualism dimension did not figure in the reward structure and GS's managers were judged on stock turnover, albeit against a different target from their UK counterparts. Bonuses were also linked to efficiency, although GS's managers had very little capacity to improve this without the ability to invest in new plant to reduce set-up and changeover times. UKP's capital criteria made investment very difficult and risked encouraging exaggerated claims of the benefits of new investments, which would then be fed through into standards with serious consequences for the ability to meet targets.

Case Study Two –
German Parent and
UK Subsidiary

6.1 Background information on the companies and the strategic motivation for the acquisition

6.1.1 Brief history of developments

GP is a project or large, contract-based engineering company based in Germany but operating in the international market where it faces two or three major competitors. The majority of its shares are owned by another German engineering company, with a listing on the Deutsche Börse (German stock exchange), which is its parent. However, the minority of shares not owned by the parent are still listed on the Deutsche Börse, an arrangement which would be very unusual in the UK, but is less uncommon in Germany.

In 1992, GP expanded into the UK. It tried to buy a UK company but failed and therefore established a UK subsidiary recruiting staff from a rival[5]. However, in the same year it acquired an existing UK repairs and maintenance firm in the same line of business. The acquired firm was small, with about 20 staff, and without a well-developed finance function. The two UK companies were effectively merged, with the subsidiary taking over the assets of the acquired company, leaving the legal shell in existence. GP paid cash in two instalments, the second linked to an earn-out, as the owners of the acquired company were kept on. Indeed one became Managing Director of UKS.

UKS did well in gaining business and had a good reputation, but was not successful in generating profit. This prompted GP to slim down UKS's top-heavy and expensive management and to install a new Managing Director (MD) in 1997. The new MD was German, had worked for a short period for GP before taking up this post and had extensive experience in the industry with GP's major German competitor. It had taken GP five years of disappointing performance before it decided to install its own man and strengthen controls. However, it should be noted that UKS is small in relation to GP in terms of staff, turnover and profit and is less significant to its ultimate parent.

6.1.2 Motives for the acquisition

There were *four* main motives in the acquisition with marketing seen as the most important.

---

[5]A major competitor acquired the UK company.

Marketing

GP was pursuing a global strategy where marketing was a key component. GP needed to expand outside Germany in order to achieve growth and one way of doing this was to have national subsidiaries in major purchasing countries. Many purchasers were national governments, or national monopolies where the change in regulatory controls had created the opportunity, but they insisted on nationally based subsidiaries. The UK is a major European market for the group's products, as well as having good links with Commonwealth countries[6].

Technical innovation

Although this is not a commodity business, cost leadership ensures competitive advantage for this industry. The cost structure of this business is dominated by material cost and this acquisition gave GP technical expertise in the use of new, low-cost materials.

Vertical integration

The acquisition also gave GP a repairs and maintenance business which was downstream from its primary large-scale contracts business. Apart from the economies or synergies of joint activity, GP also felt that having this business improved its chances of winning large-scale contracts where customers wanted an integrated service of construction and maintenance.

Diversification

There was a risk-reduction benefit in having both types of business. The repairs business was easier to obtain and had good margins thus guaranteeing a certain level of cash flow and the recovery of fixed costs.

6.1.3 Comparison of GP's and UKS's businesses

Unlike case study one, above UKS and GP are in the same line of business with large-scale contract work of several types – UKS has a sup-

---

[6]As in case study one, the parent did not formally value the option element in the acquisition. The link to Commonwealth countries was just seen as an opportunity.

porting 'after-market' of repairs and maintenance – and the core business for both is the supply of technical expertise. The acquisition can be seen as essentially a horizontal expansion into the UK when regulatory change opened up the market.

6.2 Analysis of the acquisition strategy

Each motive is considered in turn although, in this case, they are all closely interlinked.

6.2.1 Marketing

The relaxation of regulatory constraints has opened up many markets to international competition and the change in the UK created this opportunity for GP. However, in this business, national customers were looking for national production facilities and this drove the GP strategy of having a local subsidiary that was more than a 'letter-box'. Importantly, GP could not afford to have both the size and technical expertise in its production facilities in the UK commensurate with the size and complexity of the projects on offer. The success of the venture and the value available to its shareholders would depend upon its ability to pull together the resources from a number of different group companies. The conclusion is that this is a value-adding strategy providing it could be delivered by the right management controls and incentives.

6.2.2 Technical innovation

GP acquired this technical expertise through the acquisition. This particular technical expertise related to material use which was a significant component of final project cost and was not available outside of the UK. It therefore had the potential for substantial cost savings throughout the whole of the GP business worldwide.

6.2.3 Vertical Integration

There are two arguments here, one to do with marketing and the second production. First, having a repairs and maintenance business may actually alter the profile of cash flows for the project's business by making it more likely that projects will be won. Indeed by having the two businesses they can offer different product bundles from those otherwise available. Second, on the production side, there are cost reducing opportunities from designing the product with a minimum life-cycle cost. The conclusion is that there are gains to be made from this vertical integration strategy. They may not be permanent, but how long they last will depend on the nature of competition in the business.

6.2.4 Diversification

As with case study one, the issue of reducing risk through diversification arises. This is a general issue for GP, which does not solely apply in the UK. In many ways, the two arguments in case study one are to be found here. First, the standard arguments for pooling separate cash flows apply. This does nothing that investors cannot do for themselves, although its attractiveness to managers who cannot diversify in the same way as investors is obvious. Second, there are also issues about the synergy benefits of jointness and just as in case study one they have been considered under vertical integration. The conclusion here is that there is very little 'value adding' for shareholders.

6.3 The management control system and implementing the strategy

The management control system (MCS) needs to report on the marketing strategy, the extent of the benefits of technical progress and any benefits of vertical integration. The major problem facing the business is one of jointness of activities:

- how does marketing benefit as a result of having improved technical solutions?
- what effect does having a repairs and mainentance business have upon the chances of winning large contracts?

This jointness is further exacerbated by the big questions about how the group should be organised, particularly in terms of responsibility centres and transfer pricing, and other issues which relate to the interaction of group companies.

Nevertheless, the MCS can report on some basic activities. In terms of the marketing aspects of the contract business the real area of uncertainty is in winning contracts. This is a highly competitive market in which the purchasers have an interest in sharing the work around so as to ensure that the market remains competitive in the longer term. The big uncertainty is over how many contracts will be won and of what value so, at the minimum, notification of all large contracts to head office would be essential. Success in this area could relatively easily be monitored by comparing actual contracts won against benchmarks of estimated market size, market share and market chains (e.g. how much British Commonwealth business is gained through having a UK subsidiary). This would need to be done through monitoring the order book and the order book backlog, rather than through the monitoring of sales, because of the delays under German GAAP in long-term contracts feeding through into sales.

Where technical expertise is an important marketing issue, the group would want to monitor how crucial any particular expertise was in gaining contracts around the world. Similarly, where repairs and maintenance was important in product bundling then the group would need to monitor progress. For the repairs and maintenance business alone the monitoring of business won against target ought to be sufficient.

For the contracts side of the business, the major controls required would be in controlling projects, although the production uncertainties are much less than the marketing uncertainties in this type of business. Rather than placing emphasis on period profit as compared to budget, more emphasis should be placed on the control of projects to ensure that they are delivered on time and within cost estimates.

It should not have been problematic to measure the success of the policy of expansion into the UK or the economic value of having a UK subsidiary. As sales can often be obtained at the expense of profit, there would need to be clear guidelines about the extent to which this might be done to gain market share and by what time post-acquisition profitability was expected to be achieved.

Given that specialist knowledge is located with the staff in the UK a model of decentralisation would be expected to prevail, together with mutually agreed targets reinforced by suitable incentives.

It thus appears that standard budgetary control plus systems for monitoring large contracts reinforced by suitable incentive mechanisms would be enough to ensure delivery of the strategy. What causes most interest in this case is the question of how the group should be organised so as to deliver large contracts on a global basis, without unfairly impacting on the performance measures of subsidiaries and their managers' incentive arrangements.

6.4 Review of the actual management control system

6.4.1 The structure of the organisation – a matrix form

GP had previously employed a structure where its subsidiaries could be actively competing with each other for the same contracts. It therefore decided, with the creation of UKS, to establish a matrix form as its organisational structure to avoid such problems in future. The organisational style is one of financial control based upon the construct of profit centres. This matrix structure is shown in Figure 6.1.

		Activity areas				
		A1	A2	A3	A4	A5
	G1					
Geographical	G2					
subsidiaries	G3					
	G4					
	G5					

Figure 6.1 A matrix structure

On the horizontal dimension, the matrix is based upon geographically-based subsidiaries, which are set up as companies run as profit centres. The managers of these units have discretion over ordering inputs and can make capital expenditure decisions within limits pre-determined for each subsidiary[7]. This is, of course decentralisation with decision making pushed down the organisation. The vertical dimension shows the range of technological activity, with each activity having a head person based in Germany, supported by a controller, and procurement, commercial and R&D departments. Not all national subsidiaries operate in all the technological activity areas, so the matrix

---

[7]However, capital expenditure is not a big issue for companies within the group, as the nature of the business does not require huge investment in plant and machinery.

is incomplete, but it does cover the vast bulk of the company's business. To balance the matrix management structure, corporate strategy remained centralised in Germany. Here, in one location, was a team taking a view on global opportunities and possible developments.

In many ways, this matrix form is ideal given the business objectives of GP. In an early article by Knight (1976), he identified the advantages of efficiency, flexibility in scale and technical excellence with the matrix form[8]. Horizontally, each company can meet the small-scale activities of each geographical sector providing all the attributes of a small business, in particular locally based customer care. Vertically, it represents a network for the exploitation of all the firm's resources for large-scale projects, particularly government contracts, where it becomes a transnational company. For example, a major contract with a large French company to develop a facility in Latin America was led by the group's French subsidiary (acting largely as a 'letter box' for political reasons) with major inputs coming from other subsidiaries, in particular the group's US company. The contract was in US dollars, but regulated by British law[9]. Technical excellence and innovation was a feature of this UK acquisition with an opportunity to spread knowledge throughout the matrix. Finally, the matrix form has clear benefits in terms of administration and the level of staffing needed at the centre in order to make it work.

In the normal matrix form, the head of the activity for large-scale projects would have both a marketing and production role. It would be this manager who would be actively seeking the large contracts and who would then negotiate with the horizontal companies for the resources to deliver them[10]. This was not the case at GP. In fact there were important differences between the normal form and that employed by GP in the way decision rights were allocated between managers. First, it was the horizontally based managers who were, in practice, responsible for the acquisition and delivery of large projects. They were required to notify head office of any contracts bid for over a certain, fairly low, threshold (for UKS, £200,000) which varied from one subsidiary to another. The managers of the techno-

---

[8] A modern interpretation would see these as advantages of a network.

[9] This was not the only case of British law being used. It applied to most projects regardless of location. This issue of comparative advantage in legal systems was beyond the aims of this project.

[10] See Goold M and Campbell A (1998).

logical divisions were responsible for co-ordinating rather than running the contracts. The head of the division was the ultimate arbiter, subject to appeal to the board, of how a large contract should be shared out between group companies, taking account of expertise, capacity and tax considerations. Second, the horizontal managers had decision rights that enabled them to compete all round the world. That is, they were not only seeking and managing large contracts on their own territory. For example, the manager of the UK subsidiary had won a major contract to build a facility in Mexico – arguably the territory of the US subsidiary. This came through contacts with a Japanese MNC. Third, although there were local decision rights over the ordering of inputs by horizontal managers, there were corporate parameters to meet on the sourcing of some inputs. Specifically, there was a requirement to seek supply of certain specialist components on large contracts from two subsidiaries in China and South Africa. These had been set up to take advantage of cheap labour in these two countries and to produce highly specialised components. These two subsidiaries had been established as profit centres, but expectations as to the level of business activity had not been met and therefore there was a corporate requirement to put business there, moreover at a price that showed profits for them. The option to buy externally was not allowed.

This matrix structure and organisational style of financial control based on profit centres has important implications for managerial incentives and the ability to meet some of the fundamental strategic opportunities available in the network.

6.4.2 Rules on intra-group pricing

Any large contract will involve a number of subsidiaries and therefore transfer pricing is very important:

◆ The group's basic rule is that market-based prices should be used, although some business might be done on a contribution basis where there is spare capacity. Group companies have to be given the chance to meet such a price. Only if they refuse can the subsidiary buy outside the group. However, this does happen and some group companies have had to shed labour because they could not compete. As noted above, the Chinese and South African subsidiaries appear to be an exception to this rule.

◆ Market-based transfer prices may not always be readily available. UKS had recently created a synthetic transfer price by finding an equivalent but unfinished product and then costing the finishing process.

The group thus employs a sophisticated approach to transfer pricing designed to maintain competitiveness. However, the dividing line between transfer pricing and the sharing of profit on large contracts is quite hard to determine, as described in the next section.

6.4.3 Contract sharing

There are two issues here: margin sharing and risk sharing.

1. When a large contract is won, the MD has to negotiate with the head of the business area at head office as to how the work is to be shared out between group companies and furthermore how the budgeted margin is to be shared out. The focus becomes the dividing up of the budgeted margin rather than the value of the contract, since this is the portion that improves subsidiary performance. When sharing out contracts, GP takes account of capacity, as well as other factors. Tax may also be a consideration as GP can use accumulated tax losses to shelter taxable profits made in Germany.

2. The lead subsidiary on a contract bears ultimate responsibility for risk and has to monitor the work of its fellow subsidiaries as if they were third parties. Indeed, the Subsidiaries' Controller at GP felt that it actually had to be more careful, because there was always a danger that fellow subsidiaries would not be as careful on a group contract as they would be with an outside purchaser. Where there are cost overruns, one would have to determine where the fault lay to decide who was to bear the cost. If the original tender were defective, then the subsidiary leading the contract would bear the cost, but if it was inefficiency on the part of the subsidiary supplying goods or services, then the latter would bear the cost.

6.4.4 Views on the matrix structure

Views about the matrix structure varied between GP and UKS. Staff at GP had a very positive view of the structure and stressed how the strong personal links between all the managers concerned helped make the system work. However, the MD of UKS said that it created conflicts with fellow subsidiaries and deprived UKS of proper reward for its efforts, since contracts it secured would have to be shared with fellow subsidiaries, perhaps leaving it with very little margin to show for its success in winning such a contract for the group. In a recent example, UKS had to 'give away' two-thirds of the planned margin on a major contract it had won to build a facility in Mexico. There is a clash of interests between the profit centres, which want to max-imise their own profit, and the business divisions, which may base their decisions on contracts and profit sharing on other criteria. Furthermore, the business divisions are, in practice, stronger, because their managers operate from headquarters and have the final right to determine how a contract should be shared.

6.4.5 Evaluation of the matrix structure

Whilst the matrix structure makes good sense, given the internation-al project-based nature of the business, the rather arbitrary deals nego-tiated on profit sharing dilute the incentive effects of the profit-centre construct. Because each MD only cares about their benefits, this is what they compare with their effort and hence are likely to reject proj-ects that are valuable at the corporate level but not worth the effort at subsidiary level. Furthermore, although the group has a rhetoric about setting transfer prices at arms' length prices, there are strong incen-tives to manipulate these prices to extract extra subsidiary reward. The MD of UKS nevertheless feels that there is an alternative to the matrix – simply 'discipline' in tendering for contracts.

Another part of the problem for GP is the way bidding for contracts is allowed. In the standard matrix form, large contracts would be won and managed by the vertical managers. This is not the case here. It is the subsidiary managers who win and manage large contracts. Japanese multi-nationals provide a good example. The group cannot penetrate the Japanese market, but it does obtain contracts from Japanese multi-nationals for facilities outside Japan and these might be secured by many different national subsidiaries for work which is not necessari-ly in their geographical area. How the work of such contracts should be shared out between group companies and how the budgeted profit margin on the contract should be shared had clearly been a matter of contention. It is also worth noting that there is a political element in deciding which national subsidiary should take the lead on any particular contract. Clearly these are tensions that are not a consequence of the matrix form rather the way it has been implemented by GP.

6.5 Budgetary control

6.5.1 Budget formulation

The budget formulation cycle starts about three months before the year end (30 September) and is a bottom-up process, subject to review at head office, which may require improvements to be made. An English language template is provided to UKS and the same principles are used as in budget reporting. In German GAAP, the starting point is ongoing projects that are expected to finish in the year in question. The budget looks three years out – the first year in detail and broken down month by month.

6.5.2 Reporting

German head office requires monthly budget reports in a standardised format using standard account codes, which it uses to produce consolidated figures, but does not dictate how UKS should produce this data. The monthly budget report contains a balance sheet, as well as a detailed P&L based upon German GAAP. To economise on printing at head office, the budget report does not, in fact, contain the budget for the period or the year to date, as head office already has this. The scale and scope of monthly reporting reflects the needs of the ultimate parent which is short of cash and needs to present regular information to its banks. Reports are due at GP by the twelfth day after the month end and it has to pass on reports to its parent by the fifteenth day. Surprisingly, the monthly budget report sent to GP does not analyse performance by activity area.

Contact with head office is largely by telephone and through the MD. The Controller of UKS has only been to Germany once to meet key colleagues. The Subsidiaries Controller from GP will visit for a day about twice a year, but the main contact is through day-to-day queries and the monthly budget reports. This light touch control may seem acceptable now but prior to this, at a time when results were poor, contact with Germany appears to have been no stronger, and the present MD believes that inadequate control was one of the reasons why performance failed to meet expectations for so long.

There is a noticeable distinction between the time-based reports which GP requires from its subsidiaries and the project-based reporting systems which UKS uses for internal monitoring. This is understandable, as GP has to produce a consolidated report, whereas UKS needs to monitor its projects. The MD of UKS makes most use of contract reports, but has asked his Controller to provide him with a one page variance statement, explaining the differences between budgeted and actual profit for the month.

6.5.3 GAAP issues

UKS uses German GAAP essentially for all practical purposes, except financial reporting and taxation, where it relies on its auditors to make the necessary adjustments. Thus the internal and external reporting of UKS are on quite different bases and show quite different figures. For example:

♦ UKS's annual report recognises revenue and profit which are not recognised in GP's accounts until a later date. Accounting for long-term contracts makes a big difference to income recognition and stock valuation. Under German GAAP, a sale is only recognised when an order is complete;

♦ Under German GAAP, work-in-progress cannot have any profit attributed to it but anticipated losses must be provided for. Here GP and UKS have agreed to treat work-in-progress in a way which has the same numerical result, whilst being justified under different rules. In GP, a 5 per cent addition for overheads is made to the direct costs of work in progress. In UKS, a 5 per cent adjustment for profit margin is made. However, as UKS expects a considerably better margin than this, this still means some delay in the recognition of profit as compared with normal UK GAAP.

♦ There is also a difference under German GAAP where there is greater scope for warranty and such provisions. However, UKS does not make adjustments for this in preparing its budget reports under German GAAP.

6.5.4 Foreign exchange issues

Budgets for UKS are set in sterling and reported to head office in sterling so UKS has no translation exposure. Head office will translate the results into deutschmarks (DM) at a rate which is adjusted monthly.

The foreign exchange aspects of contracts are considered in section 6.5.6 (in 'Foreign currency issues on contracts).

6.5.5 Information systems

Accounting systems

GP does not require UKS or other subsidiaries to use specific accounting software, leaving this to local discretion. GP uses SAP, whereas UKS uses packages more suitable for smaller companies. Previously, it used Sage Sovereign™; now it uses Intellect™, which it finds suitable for its project-based business. For GP, common systems are unnecessary, so long as there is a common communications package. GP does its consolidation using a PC package rather than SAP R/2.

When asked about the advantages of a common system which could be interrogated on a real-time basis at head office, the Subsidiaries Controller said that, although some people might find the idea attractive, he thought that it was a bad idea. Managers need some time without head office interference to sort out problems. Furthermore, there would be a grave risk of head office interfering and demanding action where there was not really a problem at all. There was also a risk of subsidiaries developing parallel bookkeeping systems, in order to control what information was available to head office. Systems have not been used as a tool to impose control.

Communications software

This case study reinforces the lessons of the other case study that commonality of accounting software is not as important as common communications software, which GP does insist on because of the economies this brings in data processing. GP does require the use of Lotus Notes™ as a common communications package and the budget reports are sent through this medium.

6.5.6 Contract costing

Estimating costs

◆ **Contract costing** is not standardised across the group. UKS uses a simple approach. It identifies the direct costs of the project, adds allowances for financing and risk, and then adds a margin, which has to cover fixed costs as well as profit. In contrast, GP builds in more overhead costs when costing similar contracts. It adds 3 per cent to material costs to cover handling and 200 per cent on design labour. The group is not concerned about lack of comparability in costing between group companies because it is not trying to ensure that all production takes place where it is cheapest; a surprising result given the matrix design and the objective of cost leadership;

◆ **Financing costs** are calculated and added to contract costs to determine the tender price. But:
   – There is no group-wide system for determining such costs;
   – The group does not determine what interest rates are to be used; managers make their own estimates. The financing allowance at UKS is based on a rule of thumb and amounts to only 0.5 per cent of direct costs. In some cases, it may be waived, if the customer is happy to pay up-front for a lower price;
   – In all cases, contracts are designed so that stage payments cover costs (i.e. contracts are cash-flow neutral) and cash flow is shared with major sub-suppliers via back-to-back agreements;
   – These costs are not part of the project costs that have to be controlled;

◆ **A risk allowance** of 2 to 2.5 per cent of tender price is a provision against warranty claims as well as against cost overruns. When the work of delivering a contract is shared between fellow subsidiaries, this risk allowance remains with the subsidiary which is responsible for delivering the contract. This helps cover its risk as contract leader and provides additional reward if costs and warranty claims are kept under control. Once a contract has been completed, regular warranty status reports will be compiled. When the company judges that it no longer needs this provision it will be released, in some cases before the end of the formal warranty period. When the annual accounts are drawn up UKS decides how much to accrue.

Foreign currency issues on contracts

The currency in which a contract is done depends essentially upon the customer. Hence UKS is exposed to currency risk and, in particular, the US dollar. It is group policy that all currency exposure should be hedged although it does not monitor hedging activity nor insists that it is done through its own treasury department. UKS does this by:

◆ sourcing materials in the contract currency;
◆ forward cover.

In reality, UKS does not hedge all its exposure on the grounds that this is too expensive. All contract monitoring is done in sterling, using the rate used when setting up the contract to translate the figures, even where forward cover has been arranged. Any exchange gains or losses are only recognised on completion, when under German GAAP the sale is recognised.

There are several issues with this approach:

◆ The subsidiaries do not necessarily follow group policy;
◆ Cost control at the predetermined FX rate means that no account is being taken of any competitive advantage that may arise as a result of FX changes. Furthermore, the method used insulates UKS from any currency movements whilst the contract is in process, removing any incentive to respond to currency movements;
◆ Cost control in sterling is being driven by the financial reporting requirements. Any FX gain or loss is only recognised at the end of the contract – another example of the influence of German GAAP.

Contract monitoring

Contracts are monitored monthly using a reporting format which takes account of commitments and orders still to be placed to estimate the final profitability of a contract. Engineers provide data to the finance department, which prepares the reports. These reports are internally the most important part of the control system.

6.5.7 Capital expenditure approval

Capital expenditure is not a big issue as it usually concerns such things as computers and office equipment. The budget formulation process involves agreeing a capital expenditure budget, within which a subsidiary may spend. The only significant area of problem is over UKS's capital expenditure on cars for its staff. GP is unhappy, more as a matter of principle than on financial grounds, because in Germany only very senior staff get cars as part of their remuneration package. UKS is therefore looking to phase out company cars by increasing salaries. This is an interesting example of a common world-wide policy, which overrides local labour market customs and loses some tax efficiency.

6.5.8 Liquidity

The ultimate parent's cash problems do have quite an impact on the group. It has already been seen how this leads to very detailed monthly budget reports including balance sheet information. In addition, UKS had at the time of the interviews been asked to provide daily cash-flow budgets. The liquidity problem is also reflected in the management of bank accounts, which in Germany are all cleared to the centre every night. Furthermore, GP sometimes is not allowed to pay its bills, because of its parent's cash-flow position. UKS is not part of this pooling arrangement and keeps its own bank accounts. It does receive cash-flow help for the setting up of projects from GP as this is easier and cheaper than resorting to UK bank finance. There is a group wide interest rate for borrowing and lending set by the ultimate parent.

6.6 Incentive arrangements

6.6.1 Incentive arrangements to deliver the strategy

The strategic objectives examined in section 6.2 could be encouraged by the use of incentive arrangements linking bonuses to budget targets for sales and profitability. But how the targets were set would be the crucial question especially in the context of a matrix organisation with profit sharing. Aligning incentives with the critical success factors/strategic risk factors would be crucial:

◆ **Winning contracts** is the major strategic risk. So rewards to subsidiary managers based on the total value of the contract would be essential. A reward based on the profit share would only serve to dilute the incentive. A link to overall group profit might also help, although this might be too tenuous;
◆ **Subsidiary co-operation** is a key success factor of the matrix form. Rewards that did not encourage teamwork would be inappropri-

ate. Rewards for this factor could be made through discretionary elements of the total remuneration package since it would be difficult to have a well-defined measure of co-operation;

◆ **Technical innovation** is another strategic objective that should be part of the reward package. The formal recognition of the importance of intellectual property rights, perhaps through transfer payments, would act as an incentive by increasing subsidiary performance.

6.6.2 Actual incentive arrangements

The senior management remuneration scheme was introduced in 1993–94 and replaced a system of bonuses determined by the group board but unrelated to targets. The change, according to the Personnel Director, reflected the internationalisation of the company and not the matrix form. The bonus is paid as a lump sum in December and is budget-based as follows:

◆ budgeted profit of the relevant subsidiary or business area;
◆ group profit;
◆ other softer personal targets (usually not financial).

Top managers receive a fixed salary and are allocated a notional bonus element of 30 per cent of their fixed salary. Achieving 100 per cent of the targets would give the manager a 30 per cent bonus. If targets are exceeded the manager will receive a bigger bonus, but it is capped at 36 per cent of salary. Managers achieving more than 50 per cent of the target will get rewarded proportionately. Those failing the 50 per cent test, get only a minimum bonus of 20 per cent of the bonus element. This approach is applied across the group world-wide to all senior managers, although there is an acceptance that local managerial labour market conditions may affect the level of rewards required to attract and retain staff. As in case study one the incentive is applied throughout the global business regardless of any national cultural differences.

The system rewards managers partly on group profit, thus giving them some interest in overall profitability and in co-operation within the group. However, there are incentive problems between what is in the best interests of a profit centre and the group. GP had recognised and attempted to solve the problem by giving an additional reward to a subsidiary manager for the business given to other parts of the group.

The MD of UKS did not think this solved the problem because incentive arrangements for managers in the subsidiaries below the top level were based on the reported results of their profit centre.

6.6.3 Evaluation of the incentive strategy

◆ Although GP recognises the problem of individual versus joint incentives in the matrix structure its solution is only partial. Nevertheless, this is a complex issue with no easy solution. Perhaps more leverage is needed in the incentive scheme;
◆ The incentive scheme is international whilst recognising the need for differences in the level of remuneration between countries. It reflects an Anglo-Saxon style of bonus based upon hard financial criteria.

6.7 Culture: Anglo-German differences

Interviewees in both the UK and Germany were asked about Anglo-German differences. They were as follows:

◆ The level of formality in social contact with colleagues: The Germans were noticeably more formal and could not understand the compartmentalisation of relationships. This cultural difference was viewed as inhibiting openness in all levels of meetings within the business;
◆ Information available to subordinates: German managers thought they were more open with their subordinates than their British equivalents. This may reflect the fact that in Germany greater openness is required, with works councils having the right to certain information and to be consulted about certain issues;
◆ Labour contracts and relations are different in Germany: The most important body is the works council, which meets three or four times per annum. It has the right to certain information and to be consulted about certain issues. It also negotiates how the national pay deal for the sector is to be implemented locally. Labour planning has to take a rather longer-term view and terminating contracts is more complicated. If the works council does not agree, then the matter will be referred to a labour court. The MD of UKS recognised the greater labour flexibility he enjoyed in the UK, in particular in relation to using self-employed consultants. However, GP's Personnel Director claimed that most of

the time management was able to convince the works council that certain changes were needed in the interests of the company as a whole;

◆ The professional status of controllers: The German controllers were not members of a professional accounting body, but graduates, usually in Business Economics, who studied some accounting during their degree course, but learnt largely on the job. In contrast, the Controller of UKS was a chartered accountant with a relevant degree. Junior accounting staff in Germany were normally from a technical high school (Realschule) and were trained through an apprenticeship;

◆ Renegotiating contracts: Often German customers, having agreed a price, expect to alter the specification without affecting the pre-agreed price. In contrast in the UK, customers accepted that a change in the specification was likely to have financial consequences and accepted this as fair. This suggests that managers operating in different countries need to be familiar with the local style of contract management;

◆ Banking: GP's Subsidiaries Controller felt that UK banks were less able and willing to come up with tailor-made solutions than their German counterparts. He attributed this to a lack of competition in UK retail banking. Therefore GP rather than UKS arranged a great deal of the latter's financing;

◆ A different British etiquette for legal matters: The Subsidiaries Controller at GP was surprised to find that he was not allowed, in the UK, to make direct contact with the other side's lawyers, but rather had to channel everything through the company's lawyers. In Germany, there would be no problem in making direct contact with the other side's lawyers in a negotiation or dispute.

6.8 Conclusions

1. The acquisition strategy of globalisation had value. The change in national regulatory constraints had created an opportunity for global expansion. There were clear advantages from technical progress and synergies from vertical integration. A competitive advantage could be achieved by marketing the facilities and competencies of a global firm at the national level. The fact that this could not be immediately extracted was the result of poor implementation strategy and weak managerial control.

2. The due diligence process did not pay sufficient attention to management accounting systems and how control could have been implemented.

3. Change management was vital to making the acquisition work. GP initially created a top-heavy and costly board in promising seats to all the key people used to set up the company. With hindsight, making the head of the repairs and maintenance business UKS's MD had been a mistake. His expertise lay in the repairs and maintenance area, not in obtaining and running major projects, and the incentives for him to perform well had not been strong enough. Furthermore, GP had no-one groomed to go in and run the company. This action hindered success but may have been inevitable in order to create the company. Savings were eventually achieved by making the change to a two-man board – the MD and a member of the board of GP. More importantly, however, a change was made in leadership by installing a new MD with previous experience of GP and who understood its ethos.

4. It is clear from this case that although there are differences in accounting and other aspects of business practice, they were not significant in affecting the performance of UKS. The problems were much more managerial and down to a failure to implement incentives and proper financial control. In reality, adequate control mechanisms were in place, but they were not used to enforce a sufficient degree of control. For example, a group board member on the board of UKS had not pressed for targets to be met, and moreover quarterly day-long visits by the Controller from GP were not enough to unearth problems or establish control.

5. The management control system required to implement the strategy had to focus upon the following for new contracts:

   ◆ monitoring of the contract order book to assess the new market opportunities from the acquisition;

   ◆ reports on new contracts that were won as a direct result of the 'after-market' service provided by repairs and maintenance;

   ◆ reports on contracts using the new technology gained from the acquisition. GP did not consider transfer payments for intellectual property rights;

   ◆ cost control and timescale on large contracts for efficiency purposes.

For repairs and maintenance a more standard periodic budgetary control system would have sufficed.

6. Whilst it is perfectly understandable that the group should operate a budgetary control system based upon periodic comparison of budget and actuals, this arises more from the financial position of the ultimate parent than from a need for control. Periodic measurement of profit offers little of value to the managers of subsidiaries such as UKS and is also severely affected by German GAAP rules about long-term contracts.

7. It would seem that a matrix structure, although not unproblematic in its operations, is nearly inevitable in a project-based business of this sort operating on a global basis. Furthermore, the need for co-ordination of big projects, the sharing out of work in a sensible way from the group's point of view, and control over this key risk area by top management, requires that projects be ultimately controlled by head office.

8. However, the matrix structure did set up some real tensions within the group when implemented GP's way. First, the matrix model implicitly assumed that national subsidiaries will only win contracts in their own geographical area. However, this was not the case, as contacts in one country can lead to contracts gained in another, as this case study clearly shows. Second, GP implemented a profit-sharing scheme which diluted the incentives in a key success area – namely the winning of large contracts. GP offered levered rewards based on profits, but by forcing subsidiaries to give away profits much of the effect was lost.

9. The case study reinforces the finding of the first case study that commonality in accounting systems between parent and subsidiary is not essential and may not even be desirable. UKS is so much smaller than GP that it needs simpler systems. However, commonality in communication systems is valuable and leads to significant economies in processing data as well as reducing the timescales for producing reports.

10. The difference in the treatment of long-term contracts under German GAAP is more significant than one might at first imagine: it makes orders a more important performance indicator than sales;

   ◆ it means that UKS uses, for its management accounting, an approach which is quite different from that used in its financial accounts;

♦   it also has an effect on such areas as the timing of the recognition of the impact of currency movements on contracts.

11. The case study does not show much evidence of a cultural dimension as a reason for the (initial) failure of UKS. There is no evidence along the Hofstede dimensions of uncertainty avoidance or precision. The new MD adopted a team approach in managing the subsidiary but this may have been down to individuality rather than culture. GP had, after all, implemented a common reward structure across the organisation thereby ignoring the dimension of collectivism–individualism. Inevitably there is evidence of differences in the legal framework of labour markets, but they appear to have very little impact on decision making and control. The business naturally has to take a long-term focus – it is after all in the long-term contract business – which minimises the effect of the differing labour law time horizons.

Discussion and Conclusions

7.1 Corporate strategy and management accounting

In both case studies there was a clear strategy for the acquisition. Unfortunately, at the planning stage there appears to have been little active involvement by the management accounting team and, as a consequence, it took some time to achieve effective control. As this research shows, management accountants have an important role to play in clarifying, communicating and managing the strategy. It is vital that the strategic vision is shared and that proper controls are in place for the acquisition to meet the objectives set by the acquirer. There is clearly a message here for the management accountant profession.

7.2 Initial organisational control

Both acquiring companies tried to retain the management that it had acquired. There are several plausible reasons for this strategy:

◆ Local information about markets and institutions was deemed valuable. This is Bengtsson's (1992) hypothesis – that there is inevitably more dependence on the existing management team in a cross-border acquisition because of the lack of specialist knowledge. Support for this argument is clearly seen in case study two where GP set about acquiring people from a competitor in the UK;
◆ It was part of the acquisition deal in order to maintain confidence. There is some evidence for this in case study one;
◆ It was because the acquirers had no-one available to install in the acquired companies. There is some evidence for this in both case studies. In a domestic acquisition it would be much easier to impose new management, as the acquirer would have staff available who knew the business and its markets. Language is also an issue here, especially for UK companies. In case study one, UKP had no German-speaking personnel available.

However, regardless of reason, where considerable operational autonomy is afforded to a subsidiary, it would be expected that strong financial controls would be put in place, reinforced by suitable incentive arrangements. In both of these case studies this was clearly not done successfully. An alternative process of direct control by visits was clearly not feasible, as shown by the evidence of occasional visits from headquarters.

7.3 Achieving effective control

The two case studies differ in many ways and yet the evidence points to a common factor in achieving effective control. In both case studies, the failure to impose control from point 7.2 above led to poor performance being a catalyst for the belief that the key to change was a change in personnel with the parent company putting its own people in place. However, it is not clear whether the principal problem was failure to communicate the objectives of the acquisition to the subsidiary managers, or whether these managers were not properly incentivised or simply not up to the task. Certainly the lack of value in the strategy in case study one made it very difficult for the managers to show any improved performance. The strategy had to change in order for the managers to do better.

7.4 Management accounting in cross-border acquisitions

Management accounting *technology* is not an issue in either case study. The evidence is that the international firm ultimately establishes responsibility centres, sets performance measures and reward schemes, and implements planning and control mechanisms without any regard for location. However, account is taken of local conditions. For example, the hurdle rate for investment appraisal may vary because of capital market differences and the Germans may place more emphasis on engineering considerations (because of the status of engineering over finance) but this all happens with the use of the same evaluatory techniques. German rules on shedding labour also force managers to take a longer-term perspective on labour planning, but technically the same planning and budgeting procedures are used. Although technology is, of itself, not an issue what is feasible is largely driven by IT. For example, the detailed standard costing carried out now at GS would have been impossible in the days of manual calculation.

Although there is no difference in technology the objectives set for a management control system can be quite different. For example, GS's accounting systems set cost objectives at the departmental level while UKP sets them at the product level. This emphasis upon control at GS rather than decision making will be the result of a combination of environment and internal organisation. In an economically stable environment with low inflation, control of quantities rather than prices would be important especially when pricing was done elsewhere on the basis of engineering estimates. This fundamental difference had important consequences and hindered the change in objectives for UKP:

♦ Initially the difference was not immediately recognised or understood and this created misunderstanding. For example, UKP could not understand why GS attached random costs, such as breakdowns, to individual products. In the GS system this would have no decision-making consequence since the sales department employed its own staff for calculating costs for price quotations;

♦ The links between production and management accounting were weak – there was no human interaction between management accountants and production managers, and the accounting system did not link with production, as illustrated by the problem of the reporting of variances, only recognised on completion of the contracts. As a consequence, SAP R/2 could not drive the change since there were poor interfaces with other data systems – standard costing could not be implemented without the production planning and control modules.

♦ There was no great emphasis on persuading GS staff of the change. This was an important omission. This apparently simple difference in objectives drives much deeper issues of attitudes, managerial style and status. Specifically, management accountants in UKP and GS saw themselves playing different roles. With a control orientation approach, precision would be essential and there would be no need to be involved with operational and strategic matters. In contrast, a decision-making orientation would involve the use of estimates and rough-and-ready methods to produce data quickly, together with input into operational and strategic decisions. Being decision influencers would clearly affect their status within the organisation.

7.5 Foreign exchange issues

Both cases raise major foreign exchange (FX) risk issues:

♦ FX changes can be part of the acquisition strategy as shown in case study one. However, like all aspects of strategy it needs to be carefully considered right through to execution;

♦ An important issue is determining in which currency the subsidiary manager is evaluated. In both case studies, this was the local currency. This is a standard piece of evidence, but it does have consequences for how subsidiary managers behave in the light of FX changes;

◆ Subsidiary managers may face a transaction risk. GS bears relatively little transaction risk – it is an overwhelmingly deutschmark business with its other currencies effectively tied to the deutschmark. Furthermore, transfers from UKP (which have not been material) are charged in deutschmarks, thus passing the transaction risk back to UKP. In case study two, the business involves international contracts, where the customer determines the currency which will be paid. Often this is US dollars. Each individual subsidiary is responsible for its hedging within general rules which require all risks to be hedged. The primary hedging tool is physical matching of currency-buying inputs in the same currency as outputs. There is no centralisation of financial hedging despite the possibility of economies of scale and the elimination of risks by matching at group level. GP does not make the exchange rate a corporate parameter, allowing subsidiaries to make their own assessments for budgeting and contract costing purposes. UKS monitors contracts in sterling using the exchange rate used to budget the contract. Exchange gains and losses are only recognised on completion, when under German GAAP the sale is deemed to take place;

◆ Although subsidiary managers are evaluated in local currency they may still face translation risk through their incentive contracts. At some level – unit, division or group – the translation gains or losses impact upon reported profit and hence possibly upon managerial incentives. In case study one the Divisional Managing Director's bonus is based upon divisional results before year-end translation adjustments. In case study two, exchange rate movements do impact on group profit on a monthly basis, which may create some incentives for group managers to respond to exchange rate movements since part of the managers' reward is based on these. What we see is a divergence of treatment consistent with the literature. In the traditional literature, controllability focuses upon managers not being accountable for exchange rate movements which are outside their control. In the agency literature, which focuses heavily upon private incentives, risk should be 'dumped' on managers otherwise there are no incentives to take any action to avoid translation losses;

- Subsidiary managers will face economic exposure. The unexpected change in foreign exchange movements will impact upon competitiveness and therefore put their performance at risk. In the short run we expect local managers to be unable to respond to these changes (by adjusting prices or quantities), but they need not face any risk if budgets are 'flexed' for foreign exchange movements. Therefore when the exchange rate moves to a firm's advantage, the budget targets would rise to maintain the relative difficulty of meeting the budget and to ensure that managers' incentives reflect such important changes in the environment. Conversely, an adverse exchange rate movement would result in a softening of the budget. However, such sophistication is not found in either of these case studies, although sensitivity to exchange rate movements (from a translation point of view) features in UKP's updated quarterly forecasts and is likely to be a major factor in explaining sales volume variances. This risk may also explain the preference for long-term contracts written under English law in case study two. Under English law the contract could be rewritten for any changes in the project.

These are common problems for companies which operate internationally. Appendix 2 provides quarterly DM:£ exchange rates for the period 1991–98, and illustrates the amount of volatility faced – from a low of 2.206 in the third quarter of 1995 to a high of 3.098 in the second quarter of 1998.

7.6 Culture

Norms of behaviour that are culturally inculcated do play a large part in how societies behave and both case studies provide ample evidence of differences in social habits, institutions, management background, etc. between the UK and Germany. However:

- they appear to be a surmountable barrier and not a fundamental obstacle to making a foreign acquisition work;
- such differences can be viewed as 'private information' and therefore explain why acquirers are keen to retain management expertise when they buy a company abroad;
- they do not play as significant a role as private corporate incentives in explaining managerial behaviour. For example, in both case studies we see corporate reward structures being implemented across countries regardless of culture.

However, the models of culture presented here – particularly Hofstede – for the purpose of evaluating the management accounting consequences of these differences have not worked well. This may be the result of the general models themselves as outlined in section 2.4. Hofstede shows no Anglo-German difference on the *power distance index*, although the evidence in both case studies would suggest that in some significant ways power distance was lower in Germany. This was revealed in the sense of openness by German managers but not in management accounting. In management accounting one might expect power distance to be evident in the style of budget setting, i.e. the extent to which it is a top-down as opposed to a bottom-up process. Here little difference was found between the two case studies, although UKP provided more central guidance about how budgets were to be constructed. Both UKP and GP devolved a considerable amount of budget responsibility.

Hofstede also found no Anglo-German difference on *masculinity*. In management accounting this might be interpreted in terms of rewards or performance measures. There were some minor differences in incentives and performance measures but nothing significant and little that could be described as cultural. For example, UKP linked the whole incentive package to quantifiable outcomes, whereas GP did, in addition, use softer personal targets. Performance measures differed between the two case studies, reflecting the different types of business rather than national differences. Both used actual versus budget profit as the primary performance measure and as the major component in managers' rewards.

The difference on the *individualism* index is not large, although one might expect German business to be more group-focused, particularly in the area of incentive arrangements. However, these case studies present no such evidence. In fact, they show that incentive arrangements for managers are now international. German governance arrangements though clearly reflect a more consensual style of working with a greater range of stakeholder interests formally involved, including, of course, workforce representatives.

It is on the dimension of *uncertainty avoidance* that Hofstede finds the really big difference, with German managers having much lower tolerance of ambiguity. Both case studies show some differences in accounting which echo some of the findings of Ahrens (1997a,b) about the behaviour of management accountants in the UK and Germany.

There was a focus on precision – precision in contract design, evidence of a reluctance to make and use estimates, and a desire to do things the right way rather than to use rough-and-ready methods that are administratively simpler. This might be described as cultural but it could be professional. Ahrens (op. cit.) sees it as a matter of training and of the dominance of academic as against more pragmatic professional influences. Scherrer (1996) notes that the lack of an equivalent of CIMA leads to academics having a much stronger influence on what management accountants do. Of course, professional differences may be rooted in cultural norms. It may well – as is argued here – be the result of the different objectives set for management accountants to perform.

The final *long-term orientation* index was really designed to highlight differences between eastern and western cultures, but does show Germany with a slightly higher score. In management accounting terms, one might expect this to manifest itself in the area of investment appraisal, with UK companies requiring faster payback and higher returns to justify investments. Case study one certainly provides some evidence of such differences. However, differences in inflation levels, in capital markets and in strategy might also explain such differences. It is not possible to see these differences as solely cultural.

In contrast to the Hofstede model, it would appear that the differences might be more usefully explained by contractual arrangements rather than culture. Contracts include not only formal legal contracts, but also implicit understandings about how things are to be done, which may not always be part of a written contract. Differences in contractual design will clearly have consequences for managerial behaviour and management accounting.

For instance, both case studies illustrate differences in relations with customers. UKP deals largely with wholesalers in its business and is geared up so as to dispatch finished goods in its own transport as soon as production is complete. Its whole structure is geared to minimising stocks and its managerial bonus scheme rewards managers for high stock turnover. GS, on the contrary, offers its customers a stock-holding service. It produces against indicative orders and then waits for the customer to collect. Case study two offers a different illustration. The scope to negotiate extra money for changes in the specification or unanticipated problems in delivering the contract is much greater in the UK than in Germany.

There are strong contractual differences in labour markets, which are reinforced by the law. Co-determination and labour involvement in corporate governance are legal requirements in Germany. German managers know that they will have to negotiate, explain why the change is necessary and disclose a great deal of information in order to achieve change. They have to persuade the works council that change was needed in the interests of the business as a whole and, having obtained agreement, could then go ahead with the works council's support.

Lessons to be Learnt
from the Case Studies

One of the main aims of the research was to identify general lessons which other companies contemplating acquisitions abroad might use.

1. The research methodology for evaluating the cases worked well despite the many differences in the companies involved. It clearly represents a template for companies contemplating future foreign acquisitions and stresses the role of management accountants in clarifying, communicating and establishing a management control system that will achieve the strategic intent. Importantly, the case studies are exercises in how the methodology can be applied in linking the vision of the strategy to its potential value, to the key drivers for success and to its delivery by the control system.

2. It is of vital importance to have a clear and well-thought-out acquisition strategy, which is economically and culturally feasible. The acquirer then has to identify what management control systems are required to implement the strategy and consider how these can be best put in place. Case study two illustrates that there are trade-offs to be made in organisational design and incentives. Both case studies illustrate that the design of performance measures and incentives can influence the success of the strategy.

3 An early evaluation of the management team of the acquired company is vitally important. Both case studies show that both acquirers kept subsidiary management in place in the belief that local information was vital to success. This turned out not to be the case. There are several plausible reasons for this, many of which have little to do with managerial ability. It would have been better to carry out an assessment of management straight after the acquisition with a view to making any changes relatively quickly. These human resource management issues and the management of change are clearly as important as financial or accounting issues in implementing the strategy. However, managerial ability is a necessary but not sufficient ingredient. It is also essential to have a very clear and realistic vision of the purpose of the acquisition, which needs to be communicated effectively to the local managers and reinforced by incentive mechanisms and strong control systems – all of which is the management accountant's domain.

4. The analysis of the business plan and the management team are clearly important parts of the due diligence process. But this process should include:

- whatever needs to be done to enable the new subsidiary to fit into the group's existing reporting and control mechanisms;
- an investigation of the existing management accounting arrangements;
- what investment of resources is likely to be needed to establish control, and consideration of where that resource might be found;
- what changes in procedures need to be made soon after the acquisition is completed;
- a detailed investigation of the nature of the acquired business, its product range, its customers and the nature of their relationship with the company but, in particular, a good understanding of what drives costs and of how the acquired business differs from that of the parent;
- the impact of foreign exchange movements on the rationale for the acquisition;

5. Acquiring firms do need to put in some of their own staff at an early stage in order to assess management quality, understand the business fully and to help implement change. This requires resourcing, which must be budgeted for at the due diligence stage. A policy of exercising initial control at a distance based upon occasional visits and meetings does not appear to have been a successful approach.

6. There are many differences between countries in accounting procedures, management styles, language, etc. but none of these is a fundamental obstacle to a successful acquisition. Much is made of cultural differences but these do not appear to be important here. What is important is that staff on both sides need to be aware of, and sensitive to, these differences. It is important to be aware of the many institutional differences and differences in GAAP. UK managers with a German subsidiary do need to know something about the German legal rules on supervisory boards and works councils and understand the implications of the greater difficulty of shedding labour in Germany. Similarly, they need to appreciate the nature of pension provision in Germany, as well as how the liability is calculated. Conversely, German managers with a UK subsidiary need to understand the institutions and the way that business is practised in the UK.

7 Language is, unfortunately for UK companies, a problem that affects them much more than it does German companies. UKP did not have German-speaking staff to send to GS in the early stages and had no-one who could fully understand the German language reports it received. In contrast, the senior staff in GP all speak excellent English and are as at home with English language reports from UK and US subsidiaries as they are with German.

8 Good and improving IT systems are vital for success but it is not necessary to have the same system across the group. The important requirement is that all IT systems can produce accounting reports in the required format with the required information under the timetable set by the parent. There are, however, some real advantages in having systems that can communicate with each other.

References

Accountancy International, Briefing, May 1998 pp. 71–2, June p. 83.

Adollf, J, Meister, B, Randell, C and Stephan, K-D (2002), *Public Company Takeovers in Germany*, C H Beck City and Financial Publishing.

Ahrens, T (1996), 'Styles of Accountability', *Accounting, Organisations & Society,* **21**, 2/3, pp. 139–173.

Ahrens, T (1997a), 'Talking Accounting: An Ethnography of Management Knowledge in British and German Brewers', *Accounting, Organisations and Society,* **22**, 7, pp. 612–37.

Ahrens, T (1997b), 'Strategic interventions of management accountants: everyday practice of British and German brewers', *European Accounting Review*, **6**, 4, pp. 557–88.

Ballwieser, W (2001), Germany: Individual Accounts, *Transacc*, D Ordelheide and KPMG (eds), 2nd edn, Palgrave.

Bengtsson, A M (1992), *Managing Mergers and Acquisitions: A European Perspective,* Gower.

Busse von Colbe, W (1996), 'Accounting and the business economics tradition in Germany', *European Accounting Review,* **5**, 3, pp. 413–434.

Cartwright, S and Cooper, C (1992), *Mergers and Acquisitions: The Human Factor,* Butterworth Heinemann.

Charkham, J (1994), *Keeping Good Company: A Study of Corporate Governance in Five Countries,* Oxford.

Christenson, J and Wagenhofer, A (1997), 'German Cost Accounting Traditions', *Management Accounting Research,* **8**, pp 255–9.

Coates, J, Davis, T and Stacey, R (1995), 'Performance measurement systems, incentive reward schemes and short-termism in multinational companies: a note', *Management Accounting Research,* **6**, pp. 125–35.

Coenenberg, A and Schoenfeld, H (1990), 'The Development of Managerial Accounting in Germany: A Historical Perspective', *Accounting Historians Journal,* **17**, 2, pp. 288-305.

Coopers & Lybrand (1993), *A review of the acquisitions experience of major UK companies*, Coopers & Lybrand.

Crompton, A, Dorofeyev, S, Kolb, S and Meyer-Hollatz, W (2001), *European Comparison: UK and Germany*, Deloitte & Touche.

David, K and Singh, H (1994), 'Sources of Acquisition Cultural Risk', in *The Management of Corporate Acquisitions: International Perspectives,* G von Krogh, A Sinatra and H Singh (eds.) Macmillan Press Ltd.

Deutsche Börse (2000), *Fact Book 1999,* Deutsche Börse AG.

Deutsche Rechnungslegungs Standards Committee (2000), *Deutsche Rechnungslegung Standards/German Accounting Standards,* Schäffer-Poeschel Verlag Stuttgart.

Edwards, J and Fischer, K (1994), *Banks, finance and investment in Germany,* Cambridge University Press.

Foster, N (1996), *German Legal System and Laws,* 2nd edn., Blackstone Press Ltd.

Goold, M and Campbell, A (1998), *Synergy,* Capstone Press.

Gray, S J (1988), 'Towards a theory of cultural influence on the development of accounting systems internationally', *Abacus,* **24,** 1, pp. 1–15.

Grundy, T (1998), *Exploring Strategic Financial Management,* Prentice Hall Europe.

Haskins, M, Ferris, K and Selling T (1996), *International Financial Reporting and Analysis: A Contextual Emphasis,* Irwin.

Hofstede, G (1991), *Cultures and Organisations: Intercultural Cooperation and its Importance for Survival,* McGraw-Hill International.

Jenkinson, T and Ljungqvist, A (1997), *Hostile Stakes and the Role of Banks in German Corporate Governance,* Working Paper 65. 97, Fondazione Eni Enrico Mattei.

Jones, C S (1985), 'An empirical study of the role of management accounting systems following takeover or merger', *Accounting, Organisation and Society,* **10,** 2, pp. 177–200.

Kitching, J (1967), 'Why do mergers miscarry?', *Harvard Business Review,* November–December, pp. 84–101.

Knight, K (1976), 'Matrix Organisation: A Review', *The Journal of Management Studies,* pp. 111–130.

Knorr, L (1998), 'In FASB's Footsteps', *Accountancy International,* July, p. 62.

Lane, C (1989), *Management and Labour in Europe: the Industrial Enterprise in Germany, Britain and France,* Edward Elgar.

London Stock Exchange (1999), *Factfile 1998,* London Stock Exchange.

Modigliani F and Miller, M H (1958), 'The Cost of Capital, Corporation Finance and the Theory of Investment', *American Economic Review,* 48, pp. 261–297

Nobes, C and Parker, R (1998), *Comparative International Accounting,* 5th edn., Prentice Hall Europe.

Nobes, C W (1992), *International Classification of Financial Reporting,* Routledge.

Ordelheide, D (2001), Germany: Group Accounts, *Transacc*, D. Ordelheide and KPMG (eds), 2nd edn, Palgrave.

Ordelheide, D and Pfaff, D (1994), *European Financial Reporting: Germany*, ICAEW/Routledge.

Perlmutter, H V (1969), 'The Tortuous Evolution of the Multinational Corporation', *Columbia Journal of World Business*, **4,** January–February, pp. 9–18.

Scherrer, G (1996), 'Management Accounting: A German Perspective', in *Management accounting – European Perspectives*, A Bhimani (ed.), Oxford University Press.

Schneider, D (1995), 'The History of Financial Reporting in Germany', in *European Financial Reporting: A History*, P Walton (ed.), Academic Press.

Seckler, G (1998), 'Germany', *Miller European Accounting Guide*, S Archer and D Alexander (eds.), 3rd edn., Harcourt Brace & Co.

Simons, R (1990), 'The role of management control systems in creating competitive advantage: New perspectives', *Accounting, Organisation and Society*, **15,** 1/2, pp. 127–43.

Trompenaars, F and Hampden-Turner, C (1997), *Riding the Waves of Culture: Understanding Cultural Diversity in Business*, 2nd edn., Nicholas Brealey Publishing.

ULA (Union der Leitenden Angestellten) (1997), *Business Location Germany: A Compendium of political, economical and social information in English and German for persons interested in Germany as a business location*.

Warner, M and Campbell A (1997), 'German Management', in *Exploring Management across the World*, D J Hickson (ed.), Penguin.

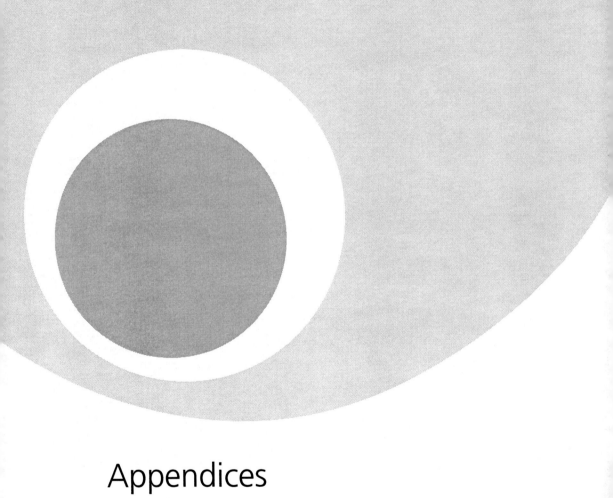

Appendices

Appendix 1 – Sources of Information about Germany

Most big four firms produce guides to Doing Business in Germany or Investing in Germany.

Charkham, J (1994), *Keeping Good Company: A study of corporate governance in five countries,* Clarendon Press.

Clarke, T and Bostock, R (1997), 'Governance in Germany; The foundations of corporate structure?' in *Corporate Governance: Economic, management and financial issues,* K Keasey, S Thompson and M Wright (eds.), Oxford University Press.

Dimsdale, N and Prevezer, M (eds.), (1994), *Capital Markets and Corporate Governance,* Clarendon Press.

Edwards, J and Fischer, K (1994), *Banks, finance and investment in Germany,* Cambridge University Press.

Foster, N (1996), *German Legal System and Laws,* 2nd edn., Blackstone Press Ltd.

Hopcroft, T (1995), *Accounting and Auditing Standards and Principles in the United Kingdom and Germany – A Comparison,* IDW-Verlag (in English and German).

Ordelheide, D and Pfaff, D (1994), *European Financial Reporting: Germany,* Routledge/ICAEW.

Randlesome, C (1994), *The Business Culture in Germany,* Butterworth-Heinemann.

Reeves, N and Kelly-Holmes, H (1997), *The European Business Environment; Germany,* International Thomson Business Press.

Seckler, G. (2001), 'Germany', in *Miller European Accounting Guide,* S Archer and D Alexander (eds.), 4th edn., Aspen Law and Business.

Union der Leitenden Angestellten (1997), *Business Location Germany: A Compendium of political, economical and social information in English and German for persons interested in Germany as a business location.*

Appendix 2 – DM:£ Spot (Mid) Quarterly Exchange Rate (1991–98)

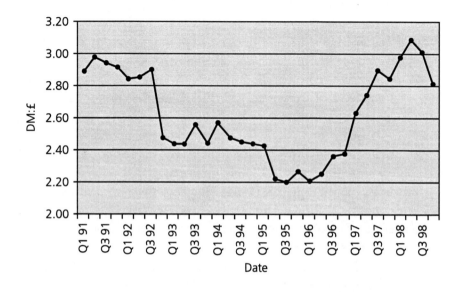

Appendix 3 – Personnel Interviewed

Personnel interviewed in case study one

UKP

1. An accountant who was involved with the original acquisition as a member of the group's M&A department and subsequently as the UK controller responsible for GS. His involvement with GS ended several years ago.
2. The current Divisional Controller in the UK responsible for GS and other subsidiaries within the Division, but only in post for about nine months at the time of interview.
3. The accountant, who was deputy for number 1 above, involved with GS from two years after acquisition until 1998. After number 1 was moved elsewhere he became more involved.

GS

1 Finance Controller at GS for the last three years.
2 Head of Management Accounts at GS since 1987, but employed there for the last 21 years and thus one of the few people in a senior position in the finance function with personal experience of the acquisition.
3 Written answers and background documents were supplied by the Geschäftsführer for Personnel.
4 The authors undertook works tours in the UK and in Germany in order to understand the nature of the business and spoke to several employees.

Personnel interviewed in case study two

GP

1. The Controller responsible for all the subsidiaries at German head office, who has held this post for ten years and therefore has a detailed knowledge of the establishment of UKS.
2. The Controller at head office responsible for the two activity divisions within which UKS operates.
3. The Manager of one of the activity divisions within which UKS operates.

4. The Manager of the other activity division within which UKS operates.
5. The Head of Personnel and Law in GP.

UKS

1. The Managing Director of UKS in post since 1997.
2. The Controller and Company Secretary of UKS in post since 1997.

Appendix 4 – Budgetary Control at UKP and GS

UKP operates a hierarchical system of budgetary reporting. GS prepares a 50–60 page monthly report in deutschmarks (DMs)[11] for its own monthly meeting; the same report is also sent to the Division. The format is substantially the same now as that used by UK members of the Division, but that has not always been the case. From it, and the other subsidiaries' reports the Divisional Finance Controller prepares a brief summary for the main UKP board.

For each business, one page of key performance indicators is provided plus a page of text, which will be presented by the Divisional Managing Director and the Finance Controller to the main board Director responsible for the division and his Finance Director via a video link. In addition to this, GS e-mails more frequent reports about production to the UK.

The budgetary reporting system is based upon a standard costing system and variance analysis. The budget is not revised, but every quarter a revised forecast for the year is made, with the revision made six months through the year being a detailed exercise. This exercise may also involve examination of the impact on the revised profit and loss forecast and the cash-flow forecast of changes in the exchange rate; e.g. making the main forecast at DM2.75=£1, but also looking at the impact of DM2.50 = £1 and DM3.00 = £1, as a way of examining sensitivities to currency movements. However, these exercises reflect only the impact of translation at different rates, rather than the economic impact of different exchange rates. Thus the budget remains the formal benchmark against which performance is evaluated. Variances are calculated against budget, but may be read and interpreted in the light of the forecasts.

GS reports in deutschmarks and has no foreign currency translation exposure as the exchange rate for translation is set by UKP as part of the budget-setting process. Any adjustments necessary are made as period 13 adjustments and are borne by the centre.

Other foreign currency transaction exposure is minimal as GS sells largely in deutschmarks, and supplies from both German suppliers and UKP are also likely to be invoiced in deutschmarks. The year is

---

[11]This case study took place before the euro was adopted in Germany.

divided into 12 four- or five-week periods; period 13 is also used for final adjustments between the management accounts and the financial accounts. However, GS reports on a calendar-month basis, which has caused UKP some difficulties in meeting the reporting timetable. Interviewees at GS claim that German companies always work to calendar months for legal reasons. It appears that staff are monthly paid, whereas many UK manual workers are weekly paid.

It should be noted that the German Commercial Code assumes that an accounting year ends on the last day of the month, whereas UK companies are allowed the leeway to move it to the nearest weekend. There also appear to be tax reasons for sticking to calendar months. Thus we appear to have a regulatory, or at least customary, difference with quite significant consequences for the UK parent of a German company. However, an alternative interpretation is that the Germans were using regulation as an excuse for not doing something they did not wish to, rather than this being a genuine barrier.

As has been stated, GS reported its figures one month in arrears. The period end date was not the only or the principal reason for this delay. It just seemed to take GS longer to produce the figures. It was only relatively recently in the history of the acquisition, with the appointment of a new Controller from outside GS, that GS's reports arrived on time. As well as being late, GS's reports were, until about two years ago, presented in German and handled at the UK end by accountants with very little knowledge of German, who just knew which figures to extract from where on a mechanistic basis. They were certainly not able to obtain much value from the narrative sections of the report.

Budget formulation starts from the sales plan, which unit product managers present to the Division's Managing Director and Finance Controller in January of each year. Once this is agreed, production is then planned in order to meet this plan. UKP supplies a central assumptions brochure, which instructs staff on which exchange rates to use, and provides guidance on the macro-environment and product markets. The budget has to be ready before the middle of February for an April to March financial year, so the timescale for budget preparation is very tight. It has to be physically presented by the Divisional Managing Director and Finance Controller to the Group Chairman. In addition to the annual budget, there is a three-year, medium-term plan for the Division, which the Divisional Finance Controller prepares with limited input from the units.

The accounting staff

The Division's finance function is small with just a Finance Controller and two staff but it does sub-contract its routine accounting work to another division. This reflects the historical fact that until recently this Division did not exist as a separate entity. In addition, each UK subsidiary has a small number of accounts personnel.

The finance function in GS is quite large in comparison, but GS is bigger and does all of its own accounting. The Finance Controller of GS is, in line management terms, responsible to the Geschäftsführer for Personnel, but deals on a day-to-day basis with the Divisional Finance Controller.

The finance function at GS is organised into three departments:

◆ financial accounting;
◆ management accounting; and
◆ industrial engineering (preparing quotations, and formerly part of the sales department);

and has about 20 staff in total.

Some of the more senior finance staff are university graduates in business economics (Betriebswirtschaftslehre), including the Controller himself and the head of management accounting. Others have trained through an apprenticeship. UKP's management accountants tended to be professionally qualified and to be members of CIMA. The divisional controller, a non-graduate, had been supported by UKP to attend an in-company MBA programme as a form of management development.

Appendix 5 – The Finance Function at GP

GP's finance function is relatively small. It has 5 controllers and a secretary to deal with its 80 subsidiaries; the German operating company has 12 accounting staff and 4 controllers. In addition the seven business divisions all have controllers, plus staff dealing with financing, insurance, bonds and letters of credit. The controllers on the whole have university degrees, usually in business economics (Betriebwirtschaftslehre). They will have learned some accounting as part of their degree course, but basically learn on the job. There is no professional body for management accountants. As in other professional jobs in Germany, such staff will commence work at a later age than is normal in the UK, as German higher education lasts longer.

The controllers are responsible for management accounting, but also for producing the annual reports. The accounting function is responsible for bookkeeping and most staff in this area will have done an apprenticeship after attending a technical high school (Realschule).

The costs of central controlling are, at present, borne by the German operating company, rather than being recharged to the subsidiaries. However, policy is under review.

UKS has a very small finance function consisting of a Controller and Company Secretary, who is a chartered accountant with a relevant degree, training with a medium-size firm of chartered accountants before moving into industry. Three other staff assist him.

Index

Accounting:
  Anglo-German differences, 7–11,
    43–4, 51, 70
  post-acquisition problems, 42–6, 55
  software, 48, 54–5, 84, 95
  systems, 71, 79
Acquisition strategy, *see* Strategy
Address form, 13–14, 51
Ahrens, T, 10, 88–9
Ambiguity, 12, 88
Analytical model, acquisition and
  management control, 29

Banks, 15–16, 77
Benefits, acquisitions, 23–4
Bonuses, *see* Incentives
Budgetary control:
  case study one (UKP/GS), 42–4,
    109–11
  case study two (GP/UKS), 69–74, 79
Business culture, *see* Cultural issues

Capital expenditure, 48–9, 73–4
Capital markets, 15–16
Case studies, 3
Case study one (UKP/GS), 31–55
  acquisition motives, 33–4
  background, 33–4
  budgetary control, 109–11
  conclusions, 53–5
  cultural issues, 49–53
  interviewees, 107
  management control system, 37–49
  strategy analysis, 34–7
Case study two (GP/UKS), 57–80
  acquisition motives, 59–60
  background, 59–61
  budgetary control, 69–74
  conclusions, 77–80
  cultural issues, 76–7
  finance function, 112
  incentive arrangements, 74–6
  interviewees, 107–8
  management control systems, 62–9
  strategy analysis, 61–2
Centralised management, 39
Change management, 53, 78, 93

Co-determination, 17–19
Collectivism, 12
Communications software, 48, 55, 71,
  79, 95
Companies, legal structures, 34
Competition, acquisition effect, 35
Conglomerate acquisitions, 24
Contracts:
  accounting treatments, 79–80
  changing, 77, 87
  costing, 71–3
  cultural issues, 15, 37, 51, 89
  management control systems, 78
  sharing, 67
Control:
  see also Budgetary control;
    Management control systems
  imposition, 83–4
  styles, 24–5
Controllers, 77, 112
Corporate governance, 16–17
Costing, 10–12, 44–6, 54, 71–3
Cultural issues, 76–7, 87–90
  acquisition problems, 24
  Anglo-German, 12–15, 49–53
  business environment, 8, 12–20
  contracts, 15, 37, 51, 89
  Hofstede's dimensions, 12–13, 88–9
  relative unimportance, 94
Currency issues, 72–3, 85–7, 106

Decentralised management, 38–9
Decision-making, 52, 84–5
Depreciation, 9
Disclosure, 9
Diversification, acquisition motive,
  34–5, 60, 62
Due diligence process, 53, 78, 93–4

Education, 19, 50, 77
Efficiency gains, acquisitions, 35,
  39–40
Employees, *see* Labour markets;
  Workforce; Works councils
Environmental differences, *see*
  Cultural issues
Ethnocentric control, 25

Exchange rates, 36–7, 72–3, 85–7
    chart, 106

Femininity, 12
Finance function, case study two
    (GP/UKS), 112
Financial targets, missed, 23
Financing, 15
Fixed assets, 44
Flexibility, workforce, 18–19, 52, 76
Foreign exchange, 36–7, 70–1, 72–3,
    85–7
    exchange rate chart, 106
Formality, personal relations, 13–14, 51,
    76
Framework, research, 29–30

GAAP issues, 7–9, 43–4, 70
Geocentric control, 25
Gesellschaft mit beschränkter Haftung
    und Co. (GmbH & Co.), 34
Globalisation, 60, 77
GmbH & Co., see Gesellschaft mit
    beschränkter Haftung und Co.

Hampden-Turner, C, 13
Hierarchies, 19–20, 51
Hofstede, G, 12–13, 49, 80, 88–9
Horizontal acquisitions, 24

Implementations, flawed, 23
Imputed costs, 10–11
Incentives:
    case study one (UKP/GS), 40–1, 47–8,
        55
    case study two (GP/UKS), 74–6, 79
    cultural differences, 20, 88
Individualism, 12, 88
Information sources, 105
Information systems, 48, 71, 79, 84, 95
Innovation, acquisition motive, 60, 61
Institutional differences, 94
Integration, 24–5, 35–6
    see also Vertical integration
Interviews, 3, 30, 107–8
Intra-group pricing, 66–7

Labour markets
    see also Workforce; Works council
    Anglo-German differences, 52
    contractual differences, 90
    legislation, 18, 94
Language, 42, 95
Legal etiquette, 77
Limited companies, Germany, 34
Liquidity, 74
Literature:
    acquisitions, 23–5
    Anglo-German differences, 5–20
Long-term orientation, 12, 89

Management, 19
    openness, 76
    post-acquisition, 53–4, 83, 93
    resources, 23, 42, 54, 94
    selection, 78
Management accountants:
    acquisition role, 29
    cultural differences, 50–1
    post-acquisition role, 85
    professional bodies, 10
    status, 50, 55
Management control systems (MCS):
    actual, 41–9, 64–9
    objectives, 84–5
    required, 37–41, 62–4, 93
Margin sharing, 67
Marketing, acquisition motive, 60, 61
Masculinity, 12, 88
Matching, accounting priority, 7–9
Matrix organisation, 64–6, 67–9, 79
MCS, see Management control systems
Methodology, research, 29–30
Model, research, 29
Motives, acquisitions, 33, 34–7, 59–60,
    61–2

Objectives, management control system,
    84–5
Organisational structures:
    Germany, 19–20
    matrix, 64–6, 67–9, 79
    post-acquisition problems, 41–2

Pension liabilities, 16, 43
Performance measures, 46–7, 88
    see also Incentives
Performance-related pay, *see* Incentives
Planning stage, management
    accountants, 83
Polycentric control, 25
Power distance, 12, 88
Precision, 50, 52
Pricing, 66–7
Professional bodies, 9–10
Provisions, 9
Prudence, 7–9

Remuneration packages, 73–4
    see also Incentives
Reporting:
    case study one (UKP/GS), 42, 46
    case study two (GP/UKS), 69–70
Research:
    acquisition surveys, 23
    background, 3
    conclusions, 81–90
    framework, 29–30
    interviews, 107–8
    lessons, 91–5
Reward systems, *see* Incentives
Risk:
    diversification, 35, 62
    foreign exchange, 85–7
    sharing, 67

Scherrer, G, 10, 11, 89
Shareholder value, 34–5, 62
Shareholders, 14, 16–17
Short-termism, 15
Software commonality, 48, 54–5, 71, 79, 95
Stakeholders, 14, 16–17
Standards, accounting, 7

Status:
    controllers, 77
    management accountants, 50, 55
Stock Exchanges, 15
Stock valuation, 43
Strategy:
    delivery incentives, 40–1
    evaluation, 34–7, 64–76
    identification, 33–4, 59–60
    importance, 93
Structures, 41–2
    flat organisations, 19–20
    matrix organisations, 64–6, 67–9, 79
Supervisory boards, 14, 16–17, 52

Technical innovation, acquisition
    motive, 60, 61
Technology, *see* Software
Transaction risk, 86
Transfer pricing, 66–7
Translation risk, 86
Trompenaars, F, 13

Uncertainty avoidance, 12, 88–9

Variance statements, 44, 45–6
Vertical integration, 24
    acquisition motive, 35–7, 60, 61–2
    management control systems, 38–9
Visits, research methodology, 30
Voting rights, German banks, 16

Work-in-progress, 9, 46
Workforce:
    see also Labour markets
    decision making, 52
    labour law, 17–19
    supervisory boards, 16–17
Works councils, 17–18, 52, 76–7